D1614672

The Collected Writings
of
W Hoste

The Collected Writings
of
W Hoste

Volume 1

Behold My Servant

Compiled and Edited
by
W M Banks

ISBN 0 946351 26 0

Phototypeset by Newtext Composition Ltd, Glasgow.
Printed in Great Britain at The Bath Press, Avon.

Foreword

Mr Hoste of London was well known in his day as a scholar of high repute. One of his outstanding contributions was his work as editor of the Believers Magazine. During that time he wrote series of articles many of which were later published in book form. He addressed matters which were of particular doctrinal significance for his day but which are still of importance in ours.

His writings bear the hallmark of a careful thinker and when refuting false doctrine he did so with biblical precision. The concise enunciation of Divine Truth was on a wide range of subjects including the Person of Christ, the infallibility of the Word, gospel and church truth and prophetic matters. Many of these tracts and booklets are no longer available and it was considered worthwhile that a new generation of believers should benefit from his written ministry.

The first volume deals with devotional matters focusing on the Person and Work of Christ. Included are the 'Passion Song of Israel', 'Divine Relations', 'Christ the Interpreter' and 'The Christ of God'. It is hoped in the will of the Lord to publish further volumes and to make available almost the full range of his writings.

A work like this could not have been completed without the help of a number of people (not to mention the constant proddings of Mr J Watson on behalf of the Publishers). In particular Mr J McCann of Brazil made available most of the material upon which the work is based. Also my son Sinclair spent a not inconsiderable time reading through some of the earlier proofs and checked the scriptural references, most of which were excluded from the original material.

Errors do inevitably creep into a new publication of this nature (and they are entirely my responsibility) but it would be appreciated that if any are found appropriate communication is made with the editor so that they can be eliminated in any further editions of the work.

The book is sent forth with the hope that many will find spiritual blessing and help through reading its pages.

W M Banks
19 Dunure Drive
Hamilton
Lanarkshire
ML3 9EY

Contents

An appreciation of
W Hoste

Preacher, Teacher, Author, Editor

By A W Phillips, London

MR W HOSTE was born to the estate of 'an English gentleman,' with every prospect of social position and worldly honour. His father was General D E Hoste, CB, late Commander of the Royal Artillery. His grandfather was Colonel Sir Geo. Hoste, CB, Gentleman Usher to Queen Victoria and Deputy Governor of Jersey.

His boyhood days were passed at his father's residence in Dover Castle, an ancient and noble pile, dating back in part to Saxon times – a building which, on account of its prominent position, attracts the attention of travellers crossing from the Continent of Europe or passing through the Straits of Dover.

He was educated at Clifton College, one of England's greatest public schools.

From Clifton he proceeded to Cambridge University, where he was a member of Trinity College, and took a theological course under the direction of Dr Handley Moule.

Brought up in a sturdy evangelical environment, it was his joy in early life to enter into the knowledge and experience of God's salvation. After graduation at Cambridge, it was his intention to enter the ministry of the Church of England, and he went through the studies necessary for ordination as a clergyman. When, however, the time drew near for his ordination he found himself unable, on conscientions grounds, to subscribe to the doctrinal formulas.

From his studies in the Holy Scriptures he was convinced that the Church of England was in grievous error on such matters as baptismal regeneration, episcopacy, apostolic succession, and the whole conception of the 'clergy' as a class among God's people distinct from the less privileged 'laity' (so-called).

Here then was the crisis of his career. What was he to do? After waiting on God his mind was made up. He must obey God rather than man. At the sacrifice of earthly prospects, valued friendships, and present gain, he determined to abandon all thought of ordination. When he left Cambridge it was to enter on a pathway of service, depending for further leading on the never-failing guidance of the Lord.

As fuller light was granted, he found that if the Holy Scriptures were to be obeyed, he must not only abandon the thought of ordination in the Church of England, but its fellowship also. Taking this further important step, it was his joy and privilege to be baptised by immersion, and to identify himself with assemblies gathered only to the Name of our Lord Jesus Christ.

Being proficient in European languages, he spent several years in arduous evangelistic labours in France, Italy, and other Roman Catholic countries.

Mr. Hoste was profoundly interested in missionary work in every part of the world. He undertook extensive tours to India and other countries for the encouragement of the workers, and made two toilsome journeys to Central Africa in days when travel in that continent was attended by dangers and discomforts almost unknown to-day.

The Lord's work in Ireland had a special place in his heart, and for many years he paid an annual visit to Belfast and neighbourhood at the time of the well-known Lurgan Conference.

Mr Hoste thus became widely known as a preacher and teacher in many parts of the world. But he was still more extensively known as a prolific writer on Biblical, evengelical, and prophetic subjects.

For about seven years prior to his death he was editor of *The Believer's Magazine.* In this service he found great delight and adequate scope for the exercise of his singular gifts as a scholarly devout and exact expositor of the Holy Scriptures. Almost to his last day on earth he was occupied with his editorial concerns and with planning the contents of the magazine.

The end came after but a brief illness. He felt that the Lord was about to call him, and when no longer able to read for himelf he asked Mrs Hoste to read to him John 14 and Rom 8. He smiled and said, 'I have no fear', and passed peacefully into the immediate presence of the Lord.

Of him it may well be said that the Word of Christ dwelt in him richly. The secret of his Christian life is in large measure to be found in the majestic words of Deut 6. 6, 7. These words, so descriptive of our brother's life and walk, are printed hereunder, together with the noble verses of Charles Wesley which are based upon them.

"THE ORACLES DIVINE"

'And these words, which I command thee this day, shall be in thine heart. And thou shalt teach them diligently unto thy children, and shalt talk of them when thou sittest in thine house, and when thou walkest by the way, and when thou liest down, and when thou risest up.' – Deut 6. 6, 7

WHEN quiet in my house I sit,
  Thy Book be my companion still,
My joy Thy sayings to repeat,
  Talk o'er the records of Thy will,
And search the oracles Divine,
  Till every heartfelt word be mine.

O may the gracious words Divine
  Subject of all my converse be!
So will the Lord His follower join,
  And walk and talk Himself with me.
So shall my heart His presence prove,
  And burn with everlasting love.

Oft as I lay me down to rest,
  O may the reconciling word
Sweetly compose my weary breast!
  While, in communion with my Lord,
I sink in blissful dreams away,
  And visions of eternal day.

Rising to sing my Saviour's praise,
  Thee may I publish all day long;
And let Thy precious word of grace
  Flow from my heart, and fill my tongue;
Fill all my life with purest love,
  Till called to join Thy saints above.

The Passion Song
of
Israel

The Passion Song of Israel

1

MESSIAH "MY SERVANT"

CENTURIES ago two Africans, a master and servant, were driving by the desert route from Jerusalem to Gaza. The former was most probably a Jewish proselyte. The fame of the Lord's House had reached him in distant Ethiopia, and, drawn by a hand he knew not, he had come to Jerusalem to worship.[1] The prayer of King Solomon was now to be answered: "Concerning the stranger, which is not of Thy people Israel, but is come from a far country for Thy great Name's sake; . . . if they come and pray in this house: then hear them from the heavens, even from Thy dwelling-place, and do according to all that the stranger calleth to Thee for" (2 Chron 6. 32, 33). The Ethiopian, like many another before and since, had gone through the prescribed rites, but had not found true peace; that, the knowledge of the Messiah alone could give. But he had procured a guide to that knowledge in a roll of the prophet Isaiah. Reading on his journey he had reached the climax of the book, the 53rd chapter, and was actually at the words "He was led as a sheep to the slaughter; and like a lamb dumb before His shearer, so opened He not his mouth: In His humiliation

---

[1] This would evidently not be his first journey thither.

2

His judgment was taken away: and who shall declare His generation for His life is taken from the earth." (Acts 8. 32, 33). Probably, while in Jerusalem, he had heard of the strange events which had lately happened there, and of the controversy which had arisen around the Name of Jesus, the Son of David. Some said this chapter referred to Him, others to Jeremiah or Josiah, or some to one yet to come.

The Evangelist and the Ethiopian. To whom and to what strange circumstances could such words apply? Suddenly a voice at his side inquired: "Understandest thou what thou readest?" (Acts 8. 30). The speaker was a wayfaring man, a Jew, who had at that moment run alongside the chariot. The Ethiopian was a great man in the world, Chancellor of the Exchequer to his Queen, Candace, but he had a further and rarer claim to greatness, he was a humble man and ready to be taught.

"How can I," he answered, "except some man should guide me?" (Acts 8. 31) and he bade the stranger come up into the chariot. There they sat, the rich man, poor in spiritual blessing; and the poor man, rich in faith and the knowledge of God. "Of whom speaketh the prophet this; of himself or of some other man?" (Acts 8. 34) asked the Ethiopian. And the other, whose name was Philip, opened his mouth and began at the same Scripture and preached unto him Jesus. The proof of a key is in the using. If it fit a good lock the chances are it was made for it. As the African listened he was convinced, like millions since, both Jews and Gentiles, that this Jesus was indeed the Messiah, the hope of Israel, the Saviour of the world. He confessed his faith, was baptised, and "went on his way rejoicing." (Acts 8. 39).

Re-examination of Messiah's Claim. Has not the time come for Jewish people to examine afresh and without prejudice the claims of Jesus, the Son of David, to Messiaship; One for whom myriads would die to-day, almost 2000 years after His death, and whom many teachers of Israel have come to recognise as the noblest of her sons and their nation's greatest glory? The Christian Gospels, containing some account of His lineage, life, and ministry, are within easy reach, and ought to be read by all. They are acknowledged, even by great scholars[2] of the world, to be masterpieces of literature, and what is more remarkable is that their authors were confessedly simple men, and not of the schools, – a publican, a peasant, a physician, and a fisherman. Whence had such men the ability to depict the most wonderful character of any age unless their hand was guided by a Higher Power? How could He of whom they wrote, who has of all men exercised the widest and most enduring influences on the human race, have been other than what He claimed to be, the Sent of God, the Messiah of Israel?

Credentials Supporting the Claim. And these claims are supported by credentials which cannot be ignored. How are we to account for the many prophecies, usually admitted by Jewish teachers, to refer to the Messiah, which were fulfilled in Him, where collusion and prearrangement were impossible? How could any one arrange to be "born of a virgin" in order to fulful Isaiah 7. 14 (see Matt. 1. 22, 23), or in Bethlehem to fulfil Micah 5. 2 (Luke 2. 4)? Was it by collusion, in order to fulfil Zechariah 11. 13, that Judas the traitor agreed with the chief priests to betray Him for thirty pieces of silver, or that the potter's field was bought for exactly that price? Was He smitten by His enemies on the cheek bone, crucified, given vinegar to drink, spat upon, His vesture divided by lot, and He "cut off" in order to fulfil Micah 4. 14; Psalm 22. 15-18; Psalm 69. 22; Isaiah 50. 6; Psalm 22. 7-9 and Daniel 9. 26? Did He arrange beforehand to die between two robbers in order to be "numbered with the transgressors," in fulfilment of Isaiah 53. 12, or to be buried by a rich man in his own tomb to

---

[2] Ernest Renan called the Gospel of Matthew the most important book ever written.

fulfil Isaiah 53. 9 (Matt. 27. 57, 60)? How did it happen that Psalm 16. 10, 11 was so accurately fulfilled in the resurrection of Jesus? Certainly His enemies did not arrange this; they did all in their power to prevent even the semblance of a resurrection. They set a seal on the great stone at the door of His sepulchre and a watch of soldiers to guard it. Did His disciples? They did not believe He would rise. Who then arranged it? Not chance, but God, whose Spirit had foretold it, "having loosed the pains of death, because it was not possible that He should be holden of it." (Acts 2. 24).

The Critics of the Last Century. One is reminded of certain critics of the last century who denied the Homeric authorship of the Iliad on the ground that to ascribe the state of civilisation, described in it, to so early a date as that of Homer was an unpardonable anachronism. Then came the archaeologist with his spade and proved the critics wrong. It is rumoured that even then they would not admit Homer wrote it, but another man of the same name who lived at the same time and place.

Equally those who deny the Messiahship of Jesus are coming virtually to admit that the true claimant was another of the same time, born in the same town and family, who lived as He lived and suffered as He suffered. "But," replies some Jewish objector, "you claim that your Messiah was the 'Son of God.' You must give up that claim if you want us Jews to accept Him as Messiah, for such a claim to our ears is monstrous; it saps at the foundation of the great essential truth of the unity of the Godhead: 'The Lord our God is one Lord' (Deut 6. 4); 'I am the Lord, thy God, thou shalt have none other gods before Me. (Deut 5. 6-7).'"

Human Sonship and Divine Sonship. Such an objection has the strongest sympathy of the true Christian. Were the said doctrine incompatible with a belief in the Unity of the Godhead no intelligent Christian could hold it. But we must remember that thoughts inseparably connected with human sonship, such as beginning, succession, separateness of essence, must be rigidly excluded from the thought of Divine Sonship. The Lord did not enter into relationship as Son by His human birth, nor even by resurrection, these only confirmed it, but "in the beginning," in eternity.

This is not a multiplying of the Godhead but an unfolding of His Being, a fuller manifestation of the Divine mode of existence. If we understand so partially our own tripartite nature – "spirit and soul and body" – in one person, who can pretend to fathom the Being of God – One, Eternal, Infinite, Absolute in three Divine Persons: Father, Son, and Holy Spirit? We only know of the Divine Being what He is pleased to reveal of Himself.

The Divine Sonship of the Messiah. "Yes," you reply, "but that further revelation is in the Christian New Testament, which we Jews cannot admit as a part of the canon of Holy Scripture." Certainly, all revelation is cumulative, and a further revelation may supplement but cannot contradict what has been previously known; the Divine Sonship of the Messiah, as revealed in the New Testament, could not be true if it contradicted the revelation of Jehovah-Elohim in the Jewish Scriptures. It is remarkable that perhaps the strongest exponent, with one exception, of this doctrine in the whole New Testament was Saul of Tarsus, himself a learned Jew, brought up at the feet of Gamaliel the elder, and deeply versed in the Scriptures and all Rabbinical learning; but it is neither John, the son of Zebedee, nor Saul of Tarsus we will interrogate, but certain Jewish prophets who lived centuries before Jesus of Nazareth, namely David, the king; Isaiah, the son of Amos, and Micah, the Morasthite. Ought not their testimony to be heard and weighed with respect? Now King David, in the second Psalm, speaks of One who is the Son of Jehovah. The Psalm at first describes an unholy alliance between the

Gentiles and "the people" against Jehovah and His Messiah, and in verse 6 gives us Jehovah's answer: "Yet have I set My King upon My holy hill of Zion." In the next verse the Messiah acknowledges this declaration and reinforces it.

Jehovah's King – Jehovah's Son. "I will declare the decree, Jehovah said unto Me, Thou art My Son, this day have I begotten Thee." Thus Jehovah's King is Jehovah's Son, the Spirit of God being witness. Does this assail "the Unity of the Godhead?" If so, it is a Hebrew psalmist[3] who does it. Later David writes in Psalm 110: "The Lord said unto my Lord, Sit Thou on My right hand until I make thine enemies Thy footstool." But all agree that Messiah was to be the Son of David, how then can David call Him Lord? Only were Messiah in divine as well as in human relationship to David "made of the seed of David, according to the flesh, and declared to be the Son of God with power by the resurrection from the dead" (Rom 1. 3-4). The same strange paradox meets us early in the prophecies of Isaiah, "Unto us a Child is born, unto us a Son is given, and the government shall be upon His shoulder, and His name shall be called Wonderful, Counsellor, The Mighty God, The

---

[3] The sixth verse quoted above is applied to the Messiah in the Midrash on 1 Samuel 16. 1, where it is said that "of the three measures of suffering, one goes to the King Messiah," of whom it is written (Isa. 53), "He was wounded for our transgressions." They say to the King Messiah, "Where dost Thou seek to dwell?" He answers, "Is this question also necessary? In Zion, My holy hill."

For non-Jewish readers it might be added that the Midrash contains the oldest expositions of Scripture by Jewish scholars, composed of Halakhah – the spiritual way, treating of customs and ordinances, and Haggadah or narrative. While the former was held in high reverence, the latter carried only the authority of the individual commentator. What is extant of the Midrash is contained in the Mishna, the chief depository of the Jewish "oral law," which forms the text of the Talmud, as distinguished from the Gemara or Commentary. The Mishna was largely collected about A.D. 220 by Rabbi Jehudah Hannasi, though probably only committed to writing in the fifth century.

7

Everlasting Father, the Prince of Peace" (chap. 9. 6). Who might this mysterious "Son" be who bears among other names "The Mighty God?" Again, do not such passages as Isaiah 41. 13 imply that Jehovah Himself would descend into the conflict with sin? "Jehovah shall go forth as a Mighty Man" ("The Mighty God" is now "The Mighty Man"). "He shall stir up jealousy like a man of war; He shall cry, yea, roar; He shall prevail against His enemies."

Who was "the Angel of the Lord!". We may also compare passages where "the angel of the Lord" and "the Lord" seem used interchangeably, *e.g.,* Genesis 22. 15, 16: "The angel of the Lord called unto Abraham out of Heaven the second time, and said, By Myself have I sworn, saith the Lord;" and Zechariah 1. 8, 17 where, moreover, the "angel of the Lord" is identified with "the *man* among the myrtles" (vv. 10, 11). In Exodus 3. 2 it is the angel of the Lord who is said to have appeared to Moses out of the midst of a bush, and in verse 6 this "angel" becomes God Himself, the God of Abraham, of Isaac, and of Jacob. See also Exodus 23. 20, 21: "Behold, I send an Angel before thee, to keep thee in the way . . . Provoke Him not, for He will not pardon your transgressions; for My Name is in Him:" expressions which show that this "Angel of the Covenant" is a Divine Person, for "who can forgive sins but God only?" (Mark 2. 7) and of what mere angel could Jehovah say "My Name is in him?"

From Everlasting *yet* Beginning in Time. Again, much later, when Herod the Great inquired of the elders of Israel where Messiah should be born they had no hesitation in referring to Micah 5. 2: "But thou, Bethlehem Ephratah, though thou be little among the thousands of Judah, yet out of thee shall He come forth unto Me that is to be Ruler in Israel." Had they not stopped there, the next sentence would have read, "*Whose goings forth have been from of old, from everlasting.*" Mysterious words! Who could that One be who was to have a beginning in time by being born in

Bethlehem of Judah, and yet had existed without beginning "of old from everlasting?"

Born in Time *yet* Before all Time. The prayer of Jesus Christ to His God and Father fits in with these dark sayings: "Father, glorify Thou Me with Thyself, with the glory which I had with Thee *before the world was*." (John 17. 5). Though born as man in Bethlehem His memory went back to a condition before time was. How came He thus to be born? The answer is contained in memorable words addressed by Jesus the Lord to a teacher of Israel who afterwards became His disciple: "For God so loved the world, that He gave His only begotten Son, that whosoever believeth in Him should not perish, but have everlasting life." (John 3. 16). He was as a "Lamb . . . slain from the foundation of the world." (Rev 13. 8).

The Unison of "Light" and "Love". Here are revealed the depths of the heart of God – "God is Light" and "God is Love." As Jehovah, in revealing His Name to Moses on the Mount, "The LORD, the LORD God, merciful and gracious, longsuffering, and abundant in goodness and truth, keeping mercy for thousands, forgiving iniquity and transgression and sin," adds words which stand out in letters of fire, "AND THAT WILL BY NO MEANS CLEAR THE GUILTY" (Exod 34, 6, 7), so the rest of the Scriptures are perfectly consistent: "Without shedding of blood there is no remission." In order righteously to pass over sin and bring forgiveness within the reach of all, God, as "Light," being in His holiness, as in all else, infinite, demands an infinite satisfaction to His broken law; and God, as "Love," provides it in the Person of His Son, the Messiah of Israel.

Both Suffering and Reigning. When Jesus of Nazareth presented Himself to Israel His forerunner, John, bare witness to Him: "Behold the Lamb of God which taketh away the sin of the world." (John 1. 29). And with this end

9

in view, as the sacrificial sin-offering, "Christ died for our sins, according to the Scriptures . . . He was buried, and . . . He rose again the third day, according to the Scriptures" (1 Cor 15. 3, 4). The central theme of the prophets is "the sufferings of Christ and the glory that should follow." (1 Pet 1. 11). How the same person could suffer and reign was an enigma. There must be two Messiahs, it was suggested, one to suffer, Ben Joseph of Ephraim, the other to reign, Ben David of Bethlehem. But is not this of the nature of an expedient?

The Holy One "Cut Off". What if the Messiah to be "cut off," according to Daniel (chap. 9. 26), should prove to be the Holy One of whom David sings in Psalm 16: "Thou wilt not leave My soul in hell; neither wilt Thou suffer Thine Holy One to see corruption?"[4] (v. 10).

"David . . . is both dead and buried, and his sepulchre is with us unto this day, therefore being a prophet, and knowing that God had sworn with an oath to him, that of the fruit of his loins, according to the flesh, He would raise up Christ to sit on His throne; he, seeing this before, spake of the resurrection of Christ, that his soul was not left in hell, neither his flesh did see corruption" (Acts 2. 29-31).

The only safe conclusion is that the suffering and glorified Messiahs are one and the same Person. The God of resurrection must be reckoned with.

---

[4] There is a remarkable comment in Yalkut on Psalm 49. 8 to the effect that the Messiah suffers in every age for the sins of that generation, but that God would in the day of redemption repair it all. But how could the glory of the Son of David repair humiliation and death to some other suffering Messiah, dead and buried years before? Only if the former should prove to be the latter raised from the dead.

2

MESSIAH – JEHOVAH – ELOHIM

BEFORE studying the 53rd chapter of Isaiah we must look at its context. Jewels lose much by being taken out of their setting. King Hezekiah was on the throne of David; they were times of reformation in Judah, but the real condition of the people remained unchanged. The words of chapter 1. 4, 6 still described them "no soundness, but wounds and bruises and putrifying sores," and this was proved by the way they followed King Manasseh in his sin and idolatry. Reformation does not suffice, nor yet restoration to the Holy Land the place of national privilege. Men need, whether Jew or Gentile, reconciliation with God and regeneration by His Spirit.

The Deliverance of Jehovah. Such a deliverance only Jehovah could grant, and in chapter 50 He chides His people for not calling on Him for it: "Wherefore when I came was there no man? When I called was there none to answer? Is My hand shortened at all that it cannot redeem, or have I no power to deliver? Behold, at My rebuke I dry up the sea; I make the rivers a wilderness . . . I clothe the heavens with blackness, and I make sackcloth their covering." (vv. 2-3). He also recalls the deliverances in Egypt and at the Red Sea. None but He could perform such wonders; but there is a greater miracle still which Omnipotence alone cannot effect – deliverance from the guilt and power of sin. For this Jehovah must assume a new role. Like the good Samaritan He must come down where the sinner lay in his misery and guilt. Accordingly in the next verses we hear Him of the mighty arm, speaking in a new character, as the obedient Sufferer and as the Comforter of the weary. "Jehovah-Elohim (literally) hath given Me the tongue of the learned to speak a word in season to him that is weary . . . He hath opened Mine ear, and I was not rebellious; I gave my back to the smiters, and My cheeks to them that plucked off the hair; I hid not My face from shame and spitting." (vv. 4-6). Jehovah is the speaker all through from verse 1, and He refers to another Divine Person, Jehovah-Elohim. How can this be explained? Only by the wonderful fact that the unity of the Godhead does not exclude a plurality of persons.

Foreshadowed in the Offerings. Again, how could Jehovah have ears to be opened, a back to be smitten, cheeks and face? Only by becoming man. And yet, marvellous condescension as this implies, it was not enough. Neither sympathy with the needy nor suffering at the hands of man could take away sins. A perfect sacrifice was needed; the antitype and fulfilment of "all the beasts on Jewish altars slain," and only Jehovah could supply this. The need of this atonement was taught by the blood of the Levitical offerings. "The life of the flesh is in the blood: and I have given it to you upon the altar to make an atonement for your souls: for it is the blood that maketh an atonement for the soul" (Lev 17. 11). The bullocks and lambs of the Jewish sacrifices must be without external blemish or spot, figurative of the intrinsic sinlessness and holiness required in the great antitypical sacrifice. To suppose that this need could be met by the sinner consuming his own flesh and blood in the act of fasting, as some have sought to explain, betrays a lack of serious thought. Could a murderer pretend to atone for His guilt by fasting? Man is a defiled sinner; how could his blood be regarded as anything but defiled even could he offer every drop of it? By fasting, moreover, a man loses flesh but not his life, and it is that which is forfeited. No man can atone for himself, nor yet redeem his brother (Psalm 49). Only God can do this, and He declares of the repentant sinner, "Deliver him from going down to the pit: I have found a ransom" (Job 33. 24), and that ransom is the blood of Him who "gave Himself a ransom for all." (1 Tim 2. 6).

"A Lamb without Blemish and without Spot". This was not accomplished by His forty days of fasting, but by pouring out His soul unto death on the cross of Calvary. It was God who made His soul an offering for sin (see Isa 53. 10, 12). Chapter 50 ends with an exhortation to the faithful remnant of Israel who fear the Lord and obey the voice of *His servant*; . . . to trust in the Name of the Lord, and stay upon their God. Who can this servant of Jehovah be who is thus placed on an equality with Jehovah? Must He not be Himself divine, the same of whom Jehovah speaks through the prophet Zechariah, "Awake, O sword, against *my Shepherd*, and against *the man that is My fellow*; . . . smite the Shepherd, and the sheep shall be scattered, and I will turn mine hand upon the little ones"[1] (Zech 13. 7)?

The Shell without the Kernel. Passing on to the ninth verse of the next chapter, we see the people of God, instead of

---

[1] A late Jewish writer tries to make this "shepherd" mean the Sultan of Turkey, because he harbours in his dominions so many "sheep of the house of Israel," and explains that Jehovah calls the Sultan "My fellow," because he (the Sultan) reckons himself as God. But even were this the case, would God condone the blasphemous pretentions of a rival? Would He whose word is "Thou shalt have none other gods but Me" recognise a false god and a false leader? The true Scriptural doctrine of the Cross of Calvary is that though Jesus was crucified by men, it pleased the Lord to smite Him on account of our sins when He hung there. On what historic occasion did God smite the Sultan? Note also how closely in verse 8 trouble to the nation of Israel follows on the smiting of "the shepherd." How well this accords with the terrible events of AD 70, following on the death of Jesus Christ and the final rejection by the people of the testimony concerning Him! Clearly, too, the smitten One is recognised by Jehovah as His own true Shepherd – "My Shepherd" – and One who can rightly claim to be His equal – "My Fellow." As there is only one God, this can only be a Divine Person existing in that unity.

13

"staying themselves on their God," plunged in distress, because deliverance is deferred. They forget that to inherit the promises patience must be added to faith. Jehovah must be asleep they think. "Awake, awake, put on strength, O arm of the Lord; awake, as in the ancient days, in the generations of old . . . Art thou not it which hath dried the sea, the waters of the great deep; that hath made the depths of the sea a way for the ransomed to pass over?" (Ch. 51. 10-11). What can be greater than the deliverances God wrought at the Red Sea? Let Him do the same now! But divine history does not repeat itself. God has some better thing in reserve – the true Deliverer, His Servant, who gave His back to the smiters, the suffering Messiah. They forget Him. They have the types without the antitype, the shell without the kernel, the form without the reality. As one has well said "Poor blinded ones, they have a lot of empty vessels, a Sabbath without true rest, unleavened bread with no real Passover, a feast of weeks and no covenant, trumpets but no joyful sound, a Day of Atonement but no atonement, booths but no sense of the presence of Jehovah, contented with empty vessels, and heaping reproaches on those who have not emptiness but the essential."

Why is Israel Judged To-day?. It is Israel, not God, who needs to awake. "Awake, awake, stand up, O Jerusalem, which hast drunk at the hand of the Lord the cup of His fury" (v. 17). Never has a people suffered like the chosen nation. Yet all avails not to put away their sins, and much less those of the Gentiles, for which some of their teachers assure them they suffer. "For all this His anger is not turned away, but His hand is stretched out still" (see Isa 5. 25; 9. 12, 17, 21; 10. 4). What, then, are the judgments for? To bring Israel to national repentance. Into what terrible national sin, then, has she fallen, "the dearly beloved of Jehovah" (Jer. 11. 15; 12. 7), to be thus left to the will of her enemies, and under the judgment of her God? Why is she scattered to the four winds and her beautiful temple destroyed? Why these ages of wanderings and persecutions? Can it be she has smitten "the judge of Israel with a rod upon the cheek?" (Micah 5. 1). Is it that she has turned her back on the greatest of all "the sons whom she has brought forth," whose[2] beautiful feet upon the mountains . . . brought good tidings of good, published salvation, and said unto Zion, Thy God reigneth?" (See Isa 52. 7). Through Him alone blessing will come to a repentant people, and it will be said in that day, "The Lord hath made bare His holy arm in the eyes of all the nations; and all the ends of the earth shall see the salvation of our God" (Isa 52. 10).

Christ as Servant. It is to this blessed Person, whom, as we saw in chapter 50. 10, Jehovah places on equality with Himself, that attention is now called in the thirteenth verse of Isaiah 52: *"Behold, My Servant shall deal prudently, He shall be exalted and extolled, and be very high."* It is generally considered that these words begin a new section. Here is one whom Jehovah calls His servant, and in whose faithfulness and ultimate success[3] He has supreme confidence. Who is He? It is true that the term "servant" is sometimes used collectively of the nation of Israel, "O

---

[2] This verse is quoted by a later writer as "How beautiful are the feet of *them* that bring good tidings" – the One preacher begets many; as the servant of chapter 52 becomes the servants of chapter 54.

[3] On the words, "He shall be exalted and extolled, and be very high," which the Targum applies expressly to the Messiah, we read in Yalkut 11 (par. 338, p. 53), "He shall be higher than Abraham," to whom Genesis 14. 22 applies; "higher than Moses," of whom Numbers 11, 12 is predicated; "higher than the ministering angels," of whom Ezekiel 1. 18 speaks. But to Him there applies this in Zechariah 4. 7, "Who art Thou, O great Mountain?" "And He was wounded for our transgressions, He was bruised for our iniquities; the chastisement of our peace was upon Him, and with His stripes we are healed." Rabbi Hara says, in the name of Rabbi Acha, "All sufferings are divided into three parts; one part goes to David and the patriarchs, another to the generation of the rebellious (*i.e.*, rebellious Israel), and the third to King Messiah."

Jacob, My servant" (Isa. 44. 1, 2), but often, as here, individually, "Behold My servant, whom I uphold" (Isa. 42. 1, 7), where "Israel" must clearly be understood as an individual member of the nation (one who Jehovah could recognised as a true "Prince with God"), for part of his work, we learn here, is to restore the nation to God (v. 5), so he cannot be the same as the nation. Surely there can only be One to whom such a service could be entrusted with hope of success – the Messiah Himself.

The Son of Man. A somewhat shallow objection has been raised that if God speaks of Christ as servant He could not also be Divine. But as has been well pointed out, "There is no difficulty in this if Jesus, though very God, became man; for as man, of course, He could become servant. The Lord never lost sight of the fact that He was God, One, not the same, with the Father; nor did He ever forget that He was "Son of Man." If a mere man had two titles, one honourable, the other lowly, he might naturally prefer the former; the Lord Jesus used the latter, "He humbled Himself." (Phil 2. 8). It was as Son of Man, in His character of servant, that He said, "My Father is greater than I," (John 14. 28) as Son of God, in His personal relationship, that He claimed equality with the Father, "I and My Father are One." (John 10. 30). But His self-humbling went much lower, even to "the death of the cross." (Phil 2. 8).

Abased yet "Highly Exalted". Jewish teachers have objected that if this be true of Jesus of Nazareth, who died like one of the lowest of the people, it cannot also be said of Him, "He shall be exalted and extolled, and be very high." Such an objection would be valid had Jesus remained dead, but falls before the Christian doctrine of His resurrection. His sufferings, too, were unique, and differed from those of the patriarchs, Joseph, David, Job, who suffered for righteousness' sake, and from those of the rebellious, which were punitive, in that His were atoning, that is, to make reconciliation for iniquity; but they are the prelude of His glory. Thus His exaltation has already begun. "God . . . raised Him up from the dead, and gave Him glory that your faith and hope might be in God" (1 Peter 1. 21), or, as another, an ex-member of the Sanhedrin, wrote, "God hath highly exalted Him, and given Him a Name which is above every name: that at the Name of Jesus every knee should bow, of things in Heaven, and things in earth, and things under the earth; and that every tongue should confess that Jesus Christ is Lord, to the glory of God the Father." (Phil 2. 11). Even those Jews who deny the future glory of Jesus of Nazareth cannot deny that He has already been exalted in one sense, seeing for Him multitudes have laid down their lives, many more to-day for Him "scorn delights and live laborious days," and to Him millions bow in worship. There are more buildings in His honour, more books concerning Him alone, than of all the greatest men that ever lived, all taken together. Is not this to be exalted? This homage is a fact in Heaven, becomes daily more so on earth, and will be so one day even in the infernal regions (Phil 2. 10, 11).

3

MESSIAH'S REJECTION AND RECOGNITION

THE prophet assured the Lord's Servant that His future recognition will be proportionate to His present rejection. *"As many were astonished at Thee; His visage was so marred more than any man, and His form more than the sons of men."* (Isa 52. 14).

The word here translated "astonished" (Heb. Shahmehm),

sometimes rendered "desolating" (Dan 8. 13), Margoliouth asserts means "to despise," to "hiss at," but the true sense seems rather to be that of wonderment (see Dan 8. 27; Ezek 26. 16), though that not always of admiration, but even of disgust. Then follows the cause of the "astonishment." (Some supply the word "saying," but is it not simpler to treat these words as an explanatory parenthesis? namely His disfigurement.) Had He come in attractive guise the world had welcomed Him, but such would have been a counterfeit Messiah. The reason of His rejection was a reason for His acceptance when He came, and the fact of His rejection should lead to His acceptance now, for this passage clearly speaks of a rejected Messiah. His very rejection then is a credential. "So shall He sprinkle many nations; the kings shall shut their mouths at Him: for that which had not been told them shall they see, and that which they had not heard shall they consider" (v. 15).

How shall He Sprinkle Nations? Moses at Sinai only sprinkled the people of Israel, but this one – a prophet like unto Moses – many nations. The "so many" corresponds to the "as many" of the previous verse, the humiliation will only find its counterpart in the exaltation. The verb *nah-zah*, frequent in the law, only means to sprinkle (*e.g.,* Num 19. 18, 19, 21), but the person sprinkled has *al* or *gl*, omitted here before "nations."

Some think it means "to sprinkle" in the sense of "to scatter words," others "to surprise," as by the sudden shock of cold water splashed on a person. This agrees with or rather perhaps suggested the Revised Version margin "startle," and certainly fits well with the *thaumsontai* of the Septuagint, though there the verse runs "many nations shall wonder."

"Regard Him with Surprised Wonder". Dr. Durell conjectures that the true reading may be "they shall regard" *ghazah* being used as meaning to look with admiration, see Psa 17. 15; 27. 4. If that be so the true translation is, "So shall many nations regard Him with surprised wonder." This will be fulfilled when Messiah returns in glory. "Behold, He cometh with clouds; and every eye shall see Him, and they also which pierced Him: and all kindreds of the earth shall wail because of Him" (Rev 1. 7). With this compare Zechariah 12. 10: "They shall look upon Me whom they have pierced,"[1] where it is to be noted that the Speaker all through the chapter is Jehovah. The "pierced" One of verse 10 is the same who, in verse 1, "stretcheth forth the heavens, and layeth the foundation of the earth, and formeth the spirit of man within him."

The Pierced One. This piercing is referred to prophetically in Psalm 22. 16, where Messiah exclaims: "They pierced My hands and My feet." How this was fulfilled in the case of Jesus need not be insisted upon, nor yet how far beyond any human pre-arrangement it all was. What other form of death but crucifixion would have ensured the piercing of His hands and feet. He had, then, to be put to death by the Romans, for stoning is the Jew's manner of execution. But there was another fulfilment of the words of Psalm 22 which occurred in a most unlikely and unpremeditated way. The Messiah hung lifeless on the cross. So clearly was He dead that it was not worth the soldiers while to break His legs. They knew His spirit had fled. But as though to make assurance doubly sure "one of the soldiers with a spear pierced His side, and forthwith came there out blood and water." (John 19. 34). He who, under the guise of humanity, was Jehovah will appear to His people, and they will look on Him whom they pierced, and a spirit of grace and supplication will be poured out on them, and "there will be a great mourning in Jerusalem; . . . the family of the house of David apart, and their wives apart; the family of the house of Nathan apart, and their wives apart; the family

---

[1] See Appendix II.

of the house of Levi apart, and their wives apart; the family of Shimei apart, and their wives apart" (Zech 12. 11-14). They will have cause to mourn. The touching scene of Joseph making himself known to his brethren (Gen 45) will be re-enacted on a greater and deeper scale. A greater than Joseph will reveal Himself to Israel, His brethren according to the flesh, and they will realise to their horror and grief that they have rejected and pierced their own precious Messiah – Jehovah Himself, manifest in flesh.

And yet, deep and terrible as this sin is a remedy will be found, and that in the most unlikely place in the universe, at the very scene of its commital. "In that day there shall be a fountain opened to the house of David, and to the inhabitants of Jerusalem, for sin and for uncleanness" (Zech 13. 1).

All their tears and mourning will not cleanse away their guilt in crucifying their Messiah, but then they will be taught the hidden meaning of His death, will believe on Him as their Redeemer, and have His atoning work in all its fullness applied to their souls. The fountain sprang first at Calvary, as has been well said, but for nearly 2000 years had run like an underground river out of sight, as far as the bulk of the nation was concerned. Now it will be opened out afresh, and these repentant ones will find complete cleansing in the Lord Jesus from all their sin and uncleanness, and as the nucleus of the New Israel will enter the Millennial Kingdom to share its glories under Messiah the Prince.

The Fountain Opened. It is in Isaiah 53 that what Zechariah calls symbolically a fountain is prophetically unfolded. Christ Himself is "the Fountain opened . . . for sin and for uncleanness." The chapter is at once a confession and a testimony. A confession on the part of true Israelites of their guilt in rejecting their Messiah, and a testimony to Him as their sin-bearer. Of course the truth of the chapter is for every one who repents of his sin, but it specially applies to the faithful remnant of Israel in the last days, who will suffer at the hands of the nation at large. How closely, too, it applies to Christian Hebrews to-day who have accepted Jesus as their Messiah and Saviour and are misunderstood by their countrymen for so doing. They plead with tears with their fellow-Israelites to believe in Him, but are treated as renegades and apostates, and accused of having forsaken their father Abraham, whereas they are now more than ever his sons and daughters seeing he is the father of the faithful. A great Jew, the celebrated Earl of Beaconsfield, was once asked whether he was a "converted" Jew. "No," he replied, "I am a completed Jew." Oh, that every one might find this glorious completeness by receiving Him who is the Antitype of all the Old Testament types, the fulfilment of every promise, and the channel of every blessing – the true Hope of Israel!

The Report – The Arm of the Lord. *"Who hath believed our report? and to whom is the arm of the Lord revealed?"* (Isa 53. 1).
Evidently the speakers have been trying to convince others of what is to them important news, but instead of a welcome they have encountered unbelief and apathy.
The "arm of the Lord" expresses His executive power, as we say "the arm of the law" – that which carries out its sanctions. It takes us back to chapter 51. 9, "Awake, awake, put on strength, O arm of the Lord."
This prayer has been heard, but in an unexpected and, to many, an unintelligible way.
"For He shall grow up before Him as a tender plant, and as a root out of a dry ground: He hath no form nor comeliness; and when we shall see Him, there is no beauty that we should desire Him." (v. 2).
The personal pronoun "He" shows that the "arm of the Lord" is a Person to whom Jehovah has entrusted His purposes. This can be none other than He of whom Asaph speaks in Psalm 80, "Let Thy hand be upon the Man of Thy

right hand, upon the Son of Man, whom Thou madest strong for Thyself" – the Messiah, the anointed One. To whom is He made known, or how? "Not to the wise and prudent, but unto babes;" not by education, but by revelation. As a learned Jew, once the bitterest enemy of Jesus of Nazareth, expressed it when describing his conversion, "When it pleased God, who separated me from my mother's womb, and called me by His grace, to *reveal His Son* in me" (Gal 1. 15); or, as Jesus Himself affirmed to another Jew who confessed Him as the Messiah, the Son of the Living God, "Blessed art thou, Simon Bar-jona: for flesh and blood hath not revealed it unto thee, but My Father which is in Heaven" (Matt 16. 17), etc.

Why Not Revealed to All?. Why does this revelation not come to all? Because so many shrink from the sacrifice it entails, little dreaming of the greater sacrifice they are making in refusing it. They cling to their "religion, received by tradition from their fathers," and refuse the Redeemer foretold by the prophets. They fear the wrath of man, who at worst can only kill the body, and they fear not Him "who can destroy both body and soul in Hell." (Matt 10. 28).

The Plant in the Wilderness. The first part of this verse describes the early years of Messiah before His presentation to Israel: "He shall grow up," or rather, "Now He grew up." The verbs are all in the past or completed tense up to verse 7, and are to be regarded as "perfects of prophetic certitude." All has been completed in the divine counsels before the foundation of the world.

To find a fragrant rose blooming in a waste wilderness would not be so great a miracle as to contemplate the moral glory of the Messiah in a world of sinners. "We beheld His glory, the glory as of the only-begotten of the Father, full of grace and truth," (John 1. 14) was the witness of one who knew Him best. The fact of Christ is the greatest miracle; to admit Him, as we must, and quibble at "incarnation" and "resurrection" is illogical.

A Branch out of His Roots. He grew up as a tender plant, without noise or outward show, but the wild beast of the field would have gladly trampled Him under foot. That such a root should grow out of so parched a soil was all to its greater honour, but to the Herods, the Pharisees, the Sadducees, the Scribes it was a noxious weed to be uprooted and destroyed. In the Karoo desert of South Africa almost the sole vegetable growth is the Karoo Bush, on which the flocks subsit, but how even this bush could grown in such soil was a mystery till it was discovered that its roots go down forty feet. The Messiah drew His supplies not from below but from Heaven. In Him was fulfilled that other prophecy of Isaiah: "There shall come forth a rod out of the stem of Jesse, and a Branch shall grow out of His roots." (Isa 11. 1). The idea is of the root of a felled tree sending forth shoots. "There is hope of a tree," as Job tells us, "if it be cut down, that it will sprout again, and that the tender branch will not cease" (chap 14. 7), and often the foliage in such a tree is treble the size of the former leaves. The house of David was this felled tree, but had not Jehovah covenanted with him that his seed should endure for ever, and the throne of his kingdom to all generations? (See Psa 89. 4). Messiah was this new shoot from the old stock. Why then was He so generally rejected? Because He was so unlike the pre-conceived idea which Israel had formed of her coming Messiah. The prophecies relating to His glory had eclipsed the humiliation foretold as preceding it. They looked for a Saviour from their earthly enemies. He came to save them first from spiritual foes; His holy life was a rebuke to their unholiness. They longed for freedom from the Roman yoke; they needed first to be set free from the yoke of sin. They hated Him without a cause, "for His love they were His enemies," but He was Jehovah's delight.

"Mine elect, in whom My soul delighteth" (Isa 42. 1), and His true people share this delight.

The Beauty of the Messiah. In the next phase of this verse the Revised Version margin has "He hath no form nor comeliness, that we should look upon Him, nor beauty that we should desire Him," which seems to suit the context, though there are notable authorities like Gesenius and Delitzsch who prefer the Authorized Version as above. The sense is not seriously affected either way. The beauty of the Messiah was not external, but moral; it did not force unwilling admiration, but attracted those who were willing to see. The same is illustrated in the "Tabernacle" in the wilderness, as we should expect, being a figure of Christ.

Exterior and Interior Views! The Amalekites and Moabites only saw the dull, dingy, badger skins of its outer covering; there was no beauty in it to them, but to the priests within how attractive must have appeared the blue, purple, scarlet, gold, and fine linen of the beautiful curtains! So to mere men of the world, there was nothing to attract in the Lord Jesus; He was very far from their carnal ideal. His lowly birth, His apparently humble parentage, His provincial up-bringing in despised Nazareth, His lack of scholastic pretentions, and indeed of every adventitious attraction, all combined to produce the effect described here. They saw "no beauty in Him"; to them He was indeed "a root out of a dry ground." But to those whose eyes were anointed by the Holy Spirit He was "the Branch of the Lord, beautiful and glorious" (Isa 4. 2), and "a plant of renown" (Ezek 34. 29). Can any good thing come out of Nazareth? asked an "Israelite indeed, in whom was no guile," for "Nazareth" was indeed "a dry ground," but when he came to Christ he saw and was conquered. "Rabbi," he exclaimed, "Thou art the Son of God; Thou art the King of Israel." (John 1. 49). One day He will be revealed in majesty, His sword girt upon His thigh, to take vengeance on His enemies, be glorified in His saints, and admired in all them that believe (Psa 45. 8; 2 Thess 1. 9, 10).

4

MESSIAH – THE SILENT SUFFERER

THAT day has not yet dawned and the next words are still true. "*He is despised and rejected of men; a Man of sorrows, and acquainted with grief: and we hid as it were our faces from Him; He was despised, and we esteemed Him not.*" (v 3).

This is no longer the experience of the speakers. Their eyes have been opened, their thoughts towards Him completely changed, but it remains true of the world. The word "rejected" should be rather "forsaken;" one from whom men held aloof, separating Him from their company. He was despised of those He honoured with His presence, rejected of those He came to bless. "A Man of sorrows, and acquainted with grief," though He ought never to have known the one or the other. The next phrase has, in one or two MSS., followed by the Septuagint and Vulgate, "his face," as though the Messiah would have to cover His face like the leper of Leviticus, and for a similar cause. To any spiritual mind such an idea has only to be known to be rejected. There is nothing to warrant it; it is in flagrant contradiction with the essential facts. Disease is a result, direct or indirect, of sin, but Messiah "knew no sin," (2 Cor 5. 21) and "in Him is no sin," (1 John 3. 5) and therefore no disease. He was "without blemish and without spot," (1 Pet 1. 19) and though His body was capable of death He was not like the rest of mankind – subject to death. His body was as incorruptible as His Spirit was impeccable. But though, or rather, because this was true of Him, the next verse is also true.

Griefs, Sicknesses, Sorrows. *"Surely He hath borne our griefs, and carried our sorrows: yet we did esteem Him stricken, smitten of God, and afflicted."* (v 4).

This verse describes one side of the Lord's public ministry. For "griefs" the Revised Version margin has "sicknesses." This is no doubt correct, as it is not really sin spoken of, but one of the results of sin, and that not by any means always the sufferer's own. This agrees with the quotation of these very words by the author of the first Gospel, "Himself took our infirmities, and bare our sicknesses" (Matt 8. 17); words fulfilled not by His "taking them," as we say, "catching them," but as the context shows by "bearing" them, in the sense of taking them away. This verse then refers to the Lord's ministry; He shared the sorrows He met in His path down here by His sympathy and relieved them by His power.

What was His motive in all this? What claim had man on His time and self-sacrifice? Certainly He did naught for gain. No one ever paid Him; only one, a Samaritan, is recorded as ever having thanked Him. It was primarily for the glory of God to reveal His heart of love. Compassion to sinners, love to His own constrained Him. Surely then men were wrong in saying.

"He was Smitten of God?". No, they were right, but the reason they alleged was wrong. They thought it was for some terrible sin of His; it was for terrible sins of theirs. He who knew no sin was made sin for us, that we might become the righteousness of God in Him (2 Cor 5. 21). This does not favour the unscriptural notion that Christ made atonement for "diseases" on the Cross; disease is not in itself sinful and needs no atonement; it is one of the effects of sin which does need atonement. But in order righteously to deal with the effects the root cause had to be dealt with. There could be no blessing, material or spiritual, in this world had Christ not made atonement for sin. It did seem that God, by forsaking Messiah, had rejected Him; it really proved He accepted Him as the Sin-offering, and treated Him as such. But though the nation misunderstood, all was clear to the faithful remnant, as their next words testify.

The Key to the Lock of Mystery. *"But He was wounded for our transgressions, He was bruised for our iniquities: the chastisement of our peace was upon Him; and with His stripes we are healed."* (v 5).

This is the key to the enigma. The righteous One atones for the unrighteous, the Holy for the unclean, the Sinless for the guilty. Is our sin viewed as the infringement of a definite commandment? "He was wounded for our transgressions." Is it regarded as something crooked or uneven? "He was bruised for our iniquities." Does it speak of guilt and enmity? "The chastisement of our peace (or which procures our peace) was upon Him." Is it looked at as a fell disease? "With His stripes we are healed."

In the next verse the two conditions are fulfilled which in one form or other, are indispensable if men are to be brought into blessing – repentance and faith.

"All" – "All". *"All we like sheep have gone astray; we have turned every one to his own way; and the Lord hath laid on Him the iniquity of us all."* (v 6).

Here we have first a collective confession of wandering like sheep on the part of all the speakers. How fitting this comparison! How like men are to sheep! It is the nature of both to wander; both men and sheep follow one another in so doing. Sheep cannot find their way back to the fold, nor men to God. But men have to admit individually what sheep have not – *responsibility*. "We have turned every one to his own way." Then follows faith in God. "The Lord hath laid on Him (Messiah) the iniquity of us all." The verse begins in Hebrew, as in English, with the same word, "ALL." The verse is entered by the first "all," enjoyed by the second. The first "all" describes those who confess their need of salvation, the second those who receive it.

As another Hebrew writer bore witness centuries later of Messiah: "Who His own self bare our sins[1] in His own body on the tree, that we, being dead to sins, should live unto righteousness; by whose stripes ye are healed. For ye *were* as sheep going astray; but are now returned to the Shepherd and Bishop of your souls" (1 Peter 2. 24, 25).

The Silent Sufferer. The prophet continues: "*He was oppressed, and He was afflicted, yet He openeth not His mouth; He is brought as a lamb to the slaughter, and as a sheep before her shearers is dumb, so He openeth not His mouth.*" (v 7).

The previous two verses have anticipated the death of Messiah; this takes us back to what preceded His death – His patient endurance under affliction, His long suffering, meekness in the presence of His people. He was led before them "unresistingly" as a lamb, He stood before them uncomplainingly as a sheep, defensible but undefended. Twice we are told "He opened not His mouth," a fact noted again and again at the trial of Jesus, and which struck His judges, both Jewish and Roman (Matt 26. 62; 27. 14). As has been remarked, "The martyrs die for what they had said, and remaining silent will not recant; He dies for what He has not said, and still is silent." It was only when directly addressed in the Name of God that He confessed that He was the Christ, the Son of the Blessed. (Mark 14. 61, 62). This was considered a final proof of His blasphemy and

---

[1] According to the Rabbis: "In the latter days the fathers shall stand up in the month of Nisan and say to the Messiah, 'Ephraim, the Messiah, our Righteousness, though we are Thy fathers, yet Thou are better than we, because Thou hast borne all the sins of our sons, and hard and evil measure has passed upon Thee, such as has not been placed either upon those before or upon those after, and all this on account of the sins of our children.'"

sufficient ground for His condemnation. But what if it be true? Oh, dreadful wickedness which can make of a true confession a ground of united and clamorous condemnation!

"By an Oppressive Judgment". *"He was taken from prison and from judgment; and who shall declare His generation? for He was cut off out of the land of the living; for the transgression of my people was He stricken."* (v 8).

The Revised Version gives "By oppression and judgment He was taken away," which makes better sense, and marks the fact that the Messiah would be cut off, not by the sudden violence (*e.g.*, of stoning), which had so often threatened His life (see Luke 4. 29; John 5. 11, 18; 8. 59), but by a judicial, though unjust, sentence. Another suggestion is, "It was exacted, and He was made answerable;" that is for what He was not responsible for in the sense of Psalm 69. 4: "Then I restored that which I took not away." But Dr. Lowth translates, "By an oppressive judgment He was taken away" (which agrees with the RV), "and[2] His manner of life who shall declare?" These last words the Revised Version translates, "As for His generation, who among them considered He was cut off?" etc. How few, if any, who were present at the death of Jesus had the slightest idea of the true reason of His death that

---

[2] In the Mishna it is written that before any one was punished for a capital crime proclamation was made in the presence of the prisoner by the public crier: "Whosoever knows anything of his innocence, let him come and inform!" (Tract, Sanhedrin Surenhus – par. 4, p. 233); on which passage the Gemara of Babylon adds that "before the death of Jesus this proclamation was made for forty days, but no defence could be found." Lowth adds, "This report, though certainly and demostrably false, illustrates the usual custom, which was omitted in our Lord's case." Our Lord seems to refer to such a procedure in John 18. 20, 21, and Paul in similar circumstances in Acts 26. 4, 5. the Gemara (discussion, complement), be it said for Gentile readers, is the Commentary on the Mishna, the text of the Talmud, the fundamental code of the Jewish civil and canonical law.

He was being stricken – "for the transgression of My people."

"Stricken – Unto Death". There is good proof that the words "unto death" were in the original text after "stricken," but seem for some reason to have been deleted by the Jews. Was it that such words correspond too closely to the death of Jesus? The early Church father, Origen, used this chapter in his controversies with the Jewish Rabbis of his day, and laid special emphasis on the additional words "unto death." Had there been a possibility of avoiding his argument by disputing the genuineness of the words they would not have failed to do so. As it was they acknowledged the weight of his argument.

Twelve Pillars – Twelve Tribes. There was a special sense in which Messiah "was stricken" for that people, whom Isaiah calls "my people," that is Israel. They were the only nation who have ever been in covenant relation with Jehovah. The twelve pillars around the altar in Exodus 24 represented the twelve tribes, and it was thus for them that the blood of the covenant was sprinkled on the altar. This blood pointed to the True Mediator of the New Covenant, Messiah Himself, yet He did not die "for that nation only, but that also He should gather together in one the children of God that were scattered abroad" (John 11. 22).

5

MESSIAH'S DEATH AND BURIAL

"*And He made His grave with the wicked, and with the rich in His death*;" (v 9) or rather as the Revised Version, "And they made His grave," or "They assigned Him His grave with the wicked."

Crucified persons were buried by the Romans, we are told, with their crosses near the scene of their crucifixion. Dr. Lowth translates, "His grave was appointed with the wicked, but with the rich was His tomb." We should note that the wicked is plural, "the wicked ones;" "rich" is singular, "the rich man;" also that "death" is plural, "in His deaths," a fact which marks the exceptional and intensive death of the Holy Sufferer "a concentrated death of countless deaths." This strange prophecy as to the burial of Messiah could not have been fulfilled by any possible collusion or pre-arrangement, but it was exactly in accord with this prophecy that Jesus of Nazareth was buried. No doubt His grave had been prepared with the two malefactors crucified with Him. How could this arrangement be overruled and He be buried in a rich man's tomb? Very few of His disciples were rich, fewer still could have had a tomb in their gardens. There was at any rate one such (Joseph of Arimathea), and his garden was adjoining the place of crucifixion; he was a secret disciple, but when confession was at its hardest he had courage to go boldly to Pilate and beg the body of Jesus. This he laid in his own new tomb, which was hewn out of the rock, "wherein never man before was laid." (Luke 23. 53). It was important that the tomb should be new, otherwise it might have been suggested, as explaining the resurrection, that some great prophet like Elisha had been buried there, and that contact with his bones had resuscitated Jesus, as in the case narrated in 2 Kings 13. 21. It is remarkable that though up to that moment wicked hands had done their worst on Him only His disciples buried Him, and those two of the highest Jews in the land, probably both members of the Sanhedrin – Joseph, the rich man, and Nicodemus, the Pharisee, a ruler and a teacher of Israel.

Testimony to His Holiness. But why should an honoured[1] grave be thus provided for One who died such a dishonoured death? It was a testimony to the holiness and truth of His walk and conversation, *"Because He had done no violence, neither was any deceit in His mouth."* (v 9).
God rewarded Him according to His righteousness, according to the cleanness of His hands hath He recompensed Him. He was holy in deed and word. To this many testified. Judas confessed he had betrayed "the innocent blood," (Matt 27. 4). Pilate again and again that he found "no fault in Him" (John 19. 4) (nor yet Herod), and his wife, too, warned him to have nothing to do with that "Just Man." (Matt 27. 19). The centurion also bore witness that He was a "righteous Man"; (Luke 23. 47) and the repentant malefactor that "He hath done nothing amiss"! (Luke 23. 41).

A Sacred Paradox. *"Yet it pleased the Lord to bruise Him."* (v 10).
Not only unjust judges laid heavy burdens on Christ, but another hand, the hand of God, laid on Him heavier burdens still. Here is a sacred paradox! We must of course divorce from the words "it pleased" any thought of pleasure

---

[1] Our Lord's burial, however, did not cease to be that of an executed criminal, because of Joseph's service of love, for leave for it was granted by Pilate himself, and the chief priests had permission from him to have the sepulchre guarded by Roman soldiers and made as sure as they could.

in the sense of complacency. We can never understand what it cost the Father not to spare His own Son, but to deliver Him up for us all. (See Rom 8. 32). Jehovah takes no pleasure in the death of Him that dieth, even of the guilty, how much less in the death of His Holy One. What is meant is that it was part of His eternal counsels, which in time God was determined to fulfil, for only by that "bruising" could blessing come to a sin-stained universe. "Bread corn is bruised" (Heb *dah-kah*) that it may become bread for the service of man. Christ was "bruised" (Heb *dah-chak*) that He might become the Bread of Life to a lost world (John 6. 33, 51). Had Messiah been only man His bruising could not have availed even for the nation of Israel; One Holy Man could at most redeem one sinful man. What sacrifice of infinite price was needed to meet the need of a world of sinners! The Redeemer must be truly man – to do the kinsman part – as the "goel"[2] and pay the redemption price, but He must be truly God in order that His redemption should be of infinite value. None but a Divine Redeemer could exhaust the claims of a Divine Avenger.

The Great Mystery of the Sufferings. *"He hath put Him to grief: when Thou shalt make His soul an offering for sin."* (v 10). We must distinguish between the sufferings of the Lord on the Cross at the hand of man and at the hand of God. Only God could inflict atoning sufferings. This is the key to the great mystery of the sufferings of Messiah. He could not reign over an unrepentant race, nor over an unredeemed people, His sufferings must precede His glory. Religious man has no conception of either the heinousness of sin or of the holiness of God. As we have seen, "God is Light" as well as "Love." God must be true to Himself. All His perfections must be safe-guarded and respected. This was

---

[2] Goel: part of goel means redeemer; followed by *dám* = avenger of blood, and then a near relative, because the right of redemption and office of avenger belong to the nearest kinsman.

so at the Cross. There "Mercy and truth are met together, righteousness and peace have kissed each other" (Psa 85. 10). But in order that God might have mercy on the sinner without compromising His righteousness, Messiah, the delight of the Father, became the forsaken of God. To the blind religous leaders of Israel a forsaken Messiah could only be a false Messiah. "He saved others, Himself He cannot save." "Let Him now come down from the Cross, and we will believe Him." "He trusted in God; let Him deliver Him now, if He will have Him, for He said, 'I am the Son of God'" (Matt 27. 40. 43). Speaking thus they unconsciouslly fulfilled Psalm 22. 7, 8 and proved His Messiahship, for this Psalm is admittedly Messianic. But why did He cry in the darkness,

"Eli, Eli, Lama Sabachthani?". At that moment He became the Antitype of every sin-offering down the ages. There He was consumed (Heb, *sah-raph*) and brought into the dust of death for the nation (see Lev 4. 21; Psa 22. 15). There He suffered once "for sins, the Just for the unjust, that He might bring us to God." (1 Pet 3. 18). Thus, though never more intrisically holy than in His death, He was treated as the sinner deserved, having "by the Eternal Spirit offered Himself without spot to God" (Heb 9. 14). Had God treated Him otherwise than He did when He hung there as the Sin-offering and the Substitute He would have connived at sin and compromised His own holiness. Consider then the infinite love of God in that it was not we who loved God, but He who loved us, and sent His Son to be the propitiation for our sins. Consider, too, His inifinite holiness, that even when His own beloved Son took the place of the guilty He did not spare Him, but inflicted on Him the full penalty due to sin. Did Christ become surety for His people? Then He must "smart for it" to the uttermost (Prov 11. 15). "God commendeth His love toward us, in that, while we were yet sinners, Christ died for us"

(Rom 5. 8). The next words reveal the glorious issue of it.

A Threefold Glory. *"He shall see His seed, He shall prolong His days, and the pleasure of the Lord shall prosper in His hand."* (v 10). Jewish teachers have objected that "seed" (*zeh-rag*) always means literal offspring, and that therefore it could not be true of Jesus that "He shall see His seed," for He had none. But how about Genesis 3. 15, when Jehovah-Elohim says to that old serpent the Devil, "I will put enmity . . . between thy seed and her seed?" Here it is not the literal seed of Satan, but his spiritual followers. Indeed the word is often used in this sense by post-Biblical writers. The seed of a religious teacher are his disciples. Even during His earthly ministry Jesus Christ saw a few disciples – about five hundred – gathered to His Person: a spiritual seed born out of due time in anticipation of His atoning death, without which He must have remained, as He tells us Himself, alone. "Except a corn of wheat fall into the ground and die, it abideth alone; but if it die, it bringeth forth much fruit" (John 12. 24). This is "the seed" foretold in Psalm 22. 30. "A seed shall serve Him; it shall be accounted to the Lord for a generation." But not only was He to see His seed, but to "prolong His days." Though "taken away in the midst of His days" He would in resurrection survive the earth and the heavens, the works of His hands (Psa 102. 24, 26). The resurrection is the keystone of the work of Christ. He "had power to lay down His life, *and* He had power to take it again." This latter was as much the command of the Father as the former (John 10. 18). By it the Spirit witnesses of the righteousness of Christ (John 16. 10). Crucified as a felon, He is justified before the universe by His resurrection, and also "declared to be the Son of God with power" (Rom 1. 4). By it, too, the believer is assured of his perfect justification (Rom 4. 25) – all his sins have been forever removed because His surety is raised – and of his own resurrection, and the world of their certain condemnation, for the One they slew has been appointed their coming Judge (Acts 17. 31).

Present Prosperity. In the meanwhile *"the pleasure of the Lord shall prosper in His hands."* What is this but the calling of repentant sinners to Himself and, especially in the present age, the gathering out of Jew and Gentile a people for His Name (Acts 15. 14; Rom 11. 5). He does not entrust this work to another, but performs it effectively by His Spirit through the preaching of the Gospel. When it is finished, the Church gathered out, the harvest of the earth garnered (there will be no ears left behind to be gleaned in that day), the next words will be fulfilled.

Future Satisfaction. *"He shall see of the travail of His soul, and shall be satisfied; by His knowledge shall My righteous Servant (lit., a righteous One, My Servant) justify many; for He shall bear their iniquities."* (v 11).

God will then repay Him in full for all His sufferings, and the joy set before Him, for which "He endured the Cross and despised the shame" (Heb 12. 2) will be His in perfect measure. This is future, the "justification of many" is a present work. The usual interpretation is the obvious one "He shall justify many" in the only true sense of justify, that is, "count righteous." But the RV margin has "makes righteous" which betrays hesitancy in the translators. Kelly translates, "By His knowledge shall Thy righteous servant instruct the many in righteousness." A reference to Daniel 12. 3 shows that this form of the verbal root must have this sense of instructing in righteousness at any rate sometimes, if not always. "They that *turn many to righteousness*" simply means *the instructors of the many* in righteousness.

"By His Knowledge". As for the expression "by knowledge of Him," is it objective that "by knowing Him," or subjective "by the knowledge He possesses?" The Hebrew idiom favours the latter. It is by His own knowledge – that spirit of knowledge which rests upon Him by which He instructs His people and leads them "in the paths of righteousness for His Name's sake." (Psa 23. 3). "The many" carries us back to chapter 52. 14, 15, "many nations," thus binding together the whole prophecy, and forward to the following verse where "the great" ought also to be "the many" and here He is said to "bear the sin of many." Notice the next words should not read "*For* He shall bear," etc., as though explanatory of the previous phrase, but "*And* He shall bear," supplementary to it. That is, besides "instructing in righteousness," which could never take away sin, He will bear their iniquities, thus effectively procuring their remission. The Messiah voluntarily takes the place of suffering, shame, and death due to the sinner, and bears the iniquities of His people. On this ground God can righteously, immediately, and eternally forgive every sinner, be he Jew or Gentile, "which believeth in Jesus." (Rom 3. 26). Nothing else could avail; nothing more is needed. "Nothing can be put to it, nor anything taken from it: and God doeth it, that men should fear before Him" (Eccles 3. 14).

The Spoil and the Strong. *"Therefore will He divide a portion with the great, and He shall divide the spoil with the strong."* (v 12).

This has been interpreted as meaning that Satan and his fallen angels will be part victors with Messiah in the age-long conflict between good and evil and share the spoils with Him, but this is a profound mistake. The powers of evil often seem to gain the victory, but their greatest victories are their greatest defeats, and when God has seemed defeated He has gained His greatest victories; the Cross of Christ proves this. Satan never has been, nor ever will be, really victor in the smallest degree; he will not reign in Hell, but be forever there the most degraded and most miserable of all the enemies of God. Dr. Lowth's translation commends itself to many: "Therefore will I distribute to Him the many for His portion, and the mighty people shall He share for His spoil." But why should the almighty Victor only *share* the spoil? Because *all* will not consent to quit the rebel ranks, and so must share the fate of the great leader of rebellion – Satan. All who surrender voluntarily become trophies of the victory of Christ and will enjoy its fruits with Him. Perhaps the "mighty people" refer to the redeemed of Israel, "the many" to the saved of the Gentiles.

6

MESSIAH'S FINAL VICTORY

ALL this proves the greatness of Messiah's final victory, which will be universally recognised alike by friend and foe. In closing, the prophet gives four reasons for this glorious result. (v 12)

1. His Life Blood Outpoured. "*Because He hath poured out His soul unto death.*" This He did when He shed His life-blood on Calvary. The sufferings of Christ were essential; "Christ must suffer," not all His works of power or words of grace could have redeemed one soul. "Without shedding of blood is no remission." (Heb 9. 22). Death must ensue. Blood coursing in the veins means life; poured from the veins death. Therefore the bread and the cup in the Lord's Supper are apart, for in it His death is shown.

The blood and water which poured from His wounded side on the Cross proved to all the reality of His death. Nor was there more room to doubt His resurrection. His body was visible, recognisable, tangible. The five scars of the crucifixion remained to prove its identity with that in which He had lived and died, though allotropically[1] modified, if the expression be allowed, by divine power.

2. Numbered with Transgressors. *"And He was numbered with the transgressors."* This was fulfilled when Messiah hung at Golgotha between two malefactors, who were probably murderers as well as robbers (see Mark 15. 7, where "who" is plural). But in a sense every man, especially of the Jewish race, "born under law," becomes a transgressor at the age of responsibility, and is in this sense "numbered with the transgressors." But Messiah was without transgression, for He observed all the commandments of God; He magnified the law and made it honourable; (Isa 42. 21), He was "holy, harmless, undefiled, *separate from sinners,*" (Heb 7. 26) and so in a category by Himself till the moment came for Him to take His place among them in His death, then "He was numbered with the transgressors." No element of humiliation was wanting. Surely to mark the uniqueness of His death it will occur alone, for God will have all other executions stayed. And if He is to die in company they must be His own disciples, faithful to death, martyrs to His sacred cause, and if the nation are to take any part in His sacrifice it will be as mourners, weeping for their Messiah at the foot of the Cross. Far otherwise was the reality. He died betrayed, denied, forsaken of His disciples, surrounded by a mocking crowd of His own nation and in company with the offscouring of the Jewish mob. Any stranger at Jerusalem would easily confound Him and them. The Friend of publicans and sinners dies between two malefactors, but carries off one as a trophy to Paradise.

---

[1] "Allotropy" is the property possessed by certain elemental substances, such as carbon, oxygen, sulphur, phosphorus, of existing under different conditions or modifications, and exhibiting distinct physical and chemical properties.

3. The Divine Sin-Bearer. "*He bare the sins of many.*" This is a third reason for His exaltation. Some would have us believe that Christ died merely as an example of self-sacrifice. But the essence of self-sacrifice is that there is some one needing rescue. To jump into a stormy sea in which no one is drowning, to rush into a conflagration where no one is in danger of burning, would be the act of a fool or a suicide. Christ did not go to the Cross merely as an example of self-sacrifice, though He was that, but to save sinners from the judgment due to them. Thus it was that, as the Substitute, "He bore the sins of many." This is abhorrent to the self-righteous religionist or moralist; to the convicted sinner it brings pardon and peace.

It is well to notice the word "many." Christ gave Himself a ransom for all" (1 Tim 2. 6), but when it is a question of sin-bearing it was for "many." "Christ was once offered to bear the sins of many" (Heb 9. 28). That death was sufficient for all, efficient for many. Potentially for the whole race, it was only effective for those who believe. As Surety of the New Covenant He became Himself the Covenant victim, and bare the sins of the Covenant people.

It is always thus that sin-bearing is viewed in the Scripture. On the great Day of Atonement there were two goats. The first was slain and its blood carried by the High Priest into the Holy of Holies and sprinkled once on the mercy-seat and seven times before it. That was a secret transaction between Jehovah and the High Priest, and though on this occasion the Atonement only touched the people of Israel, yet in the antitype, when Christ was offered up as the Atonement for sin, His work had the whole human race in view and not a single member of humanity, but was potentially affected thereby. Provision was made for all. God can now righteously, without the compromise of a single holy claim, stretch forth His hands in grace to every sinner. But when the blood of the first goat had been disposed of, then the other – the scape-goat (*azazel,* lit., the goat of departure) – was taken, and Aaron laid his hands on its head and confessed over it all the *iniquities of the children of Israel,* and all *their* transgressions in all *their* sins, *putting them upon the head of the goat,* and then sent him away by the hand of a fit man into the wilderness, and the goat bore upon him all *their* iniquities into a land not inhabited, and was let go into the wilderness (Lev 16). The blood in the Holiest met the claims of God; the scapegoat bearing away their sins met the needs of the people of God. When a sinner believes in Christ he is let into a family secret: "all his sins were borne on Calvary."

The word translated "not inhabited" (Lev 16. 22) is more correctly, as in margin, "of separation." It occurs in 2 Chronicles 26. 21 with reference to the "cutting-off" of Uzziah, the leper king, from the house of the Lord, and is used in verse 8 of our chapter: "He was *cut off* out of the land of the living." The High Priest did return to testify that in virtue of the sprinkled blood he had seen the face of God and lived; the scapegoat never returned, and so the sins it bore were typically gone for ever. The great Day of Atonement found its antitypical fulfilment when Christ was slain almost 2000 years ago. Strictly speaking, the first part of the Day is being enacted in this age; the High Priest is in the Holiest, and His priestly family are waiting for Him to come forth and receive them unto Himself; the scapegoat aspect of His work will only be carried out when the remnant of Israel repents as a nation. Then they will understand that Messiah, as the Sacrificial Victim, has borne their sins away. Indeed the sins of all who believe are already "removed as far as the east is from the west" (Psa 103. 12); "made white as snow" (Isa 1. 18); "blotted out as a thick cloud" (Isa 44. 22); "cast behind God's back" (Isa 38. 17); "cast into the depths of the sea" (Micah 7. 19); "forgiven and remembered no more" (Jer 31. 34).

4. Intercession for the Transgressors. *"And made intercession for the transgressors."* These words were nobly illustrated in the prayer of "Messiah," "Father, forgive them, for they know not what they do" (Luke 23. 24). The context would show that those specially included in the prayer were the Roman Centurion and soldiers, who completed the act of crucifixion. The prayer was that very day answered by their conversion (see Matt 27. 54; Mark 15. 39; Luke 23. 47). But it was fulfilled in a broader sense at Pentecost, though not exhausted even then.[2] It has been going on ever since. Christ is still making intercession for the transgressors, and all the day stretching forth His hands to a disobedient and gain-saying people (Isa 65. 2), who for their sins have been for "many days," as Hosea foretold, "without a king . . . and without a sacrifice, and without an image" (chap 3. 4). But even from them God is calling out a remnant according to the election of grace (Rom 11. 5), and visiting "the Gentiles to take out of them a people for His Name" (Acts 15. 14), to form together "the Church which is His Body." But "when the Redeemer shall come to Zion and unto them that turn from transgression in Jacob" (Isa 59. 20), "afterward shall the children of Israel return, and seek the Lord their God, and David their king; and shall fear the Lord and His goodness in the latter days" (Hos 3. 5).

---

[2] The future is used with *vav* conversive, instead of the preterite as elsewhere, to mark the fact that the act, though begun, is not yet completed.

Appendix 1

THE DUAL AUTHORSHIP OF ISAIAH

THE theory of the Higher Critics as to the double or multiple authorship of the Book of "Isaiah" originated, it would seem, in their premise that there is no such thing in the Bible as

Prophecy in the Sense of Prediction. To allow this would be to admit the miraculous; in their eyes a *reductio ad absurdum*. A certain notorious destructive critic wrote: "It is now commonly admitted (a typical phrase of these writers, which is convenient as assuming what has to be proved) that the essential part of Biblical prophecy does not lie in predicting contingent events ... In no prophecy can it be shown that literal predicting of distant historical events is contained." Another affirms, "The prophets never predict far remote events." Why this emphasis, "far remote?" Is it conceded they could predict a year, or even a month, ahead? Would not this be miraculous and include the possibility of the greater? According to these teachers the Old Testament prophets philosophised on passing or past events; never predicted the future. By this showing we may all be prophets. It is not difficult to-day to foretell yesterday's weather. But someone will exclaim, "No prediction in the Old Testament prophecies!" What do the Critics make of the Messianic prophecies? Deny there are any! What of the predictions as to the destruction of Babylon, etc? Postdate their pronouncement. What of the promises of restoration to Israel? Antedate their fulfilment! It will be sufficient for any Christian, who has the fear of God, to remember that our Lord again and again applied Old Testament prophecies to Himself (*e.g.,* Mark 14. 2;

Luke 24. 27, 44; John 5. 46), and this, too, in a very marked way after His resurrection.

Are the Critics Ever Wrong?. However, the theories of the critics must be upheld at any cost. Scriptures, like the Book of Daniel, or the section of Isaiah now in question, which profess to contain a detaild account of future events must be brought down to a date subsequent to those events. The logical deduction, then, would be that large parts of these prophecies have not yet been written at all, for it is certain that some of the events foretold in them are still future. When, to quote only one intance, has Mount Zion been established in the top of the mountains, or have all nations flown like rivers to it? Have swords yet been beaten into plowshares, and spears into pruninghooks? (Isa 2. 2, 4). This was still future during the last war, and certain pessimists doubt if it be very near even to-day.

Profitable Forgeries! Forgeries are not edifying documents, but according to the destructive critics the prophecies through forgeries are profitable for all that. The morality of the Scriptures would not be of a high order if forged documents, universally held in contempt by honourable men, could yet edify according to its standard.

The Jews, however, who may be supposed to know most of their own national writings, were never aware of two or more Isaiahs. They received the book from their fathers as the work of one author; Josephus, the national historian, only knew of one Isaiah; and Ben Sira, in Ecclesiastes 48. 2, refers to the opening words of Isaiah 40 as by "Isaiah." The "Modernists," however, know better. They are quite sure they are right. They have strong *subjective* reasons for feeling this. It is as though a society of Chinese mandarins passed a resolution that the "Idylls of the King" were written before the "Canterbury Tales" on the ground that King Arthur lived before Richard II. It would raise a smile but convince nobody. Are not the Jews of our Lord's time, being nearer the source of their own writings, less likely to be imposed upon by forgeries than modern critics by the exigencies of their pet theories?

Arguments Amissing! The Higher Critics affirm, "as clear to a child," that chapters 1-39 of the Collection called "Isaiah" are addressed to Israel in Jerusalem, and chapters 40-66, "as clearly as words can state it," to Israel in Babylon. It is not an unknown device in controversy, when arguments are scarce, to vouch that none are needed. Neither of the above statements however are well founded. Chapters 13 and 14,[1] as has been well pointed out, refer distinctly to the fall of Babylon. In the 40th chapter, on the other hand, we read in verse 2, "Speak ye comfortably to Jerusalem," and again in verse 9, "O Zion . . . get thee up into the high mountain; O Jerusalem . . . lift up thy voice with strength." How can such words be meant for Israel in Babylon when they are addressed elsewhere? These must be, I suppose, the interpolations of yet another Isaiah. It reminds one of the cycles and epicycles of the Ptolemaic system invented for the occasion. As has been well said: "Any wild theory can be 'proved' if one may simply blot out, without rhyme or reason, all the opposing evidence." The "modernist" proof of the late date of Daniel is largely a philological one based on certain Greek words, but the Elephantine papyri, carefully dated, have shown these words were used at the traditional date of Daniel. Had these words been against the modernist view they would long ago have been brushed aside as "undoubted interpolations."

"A People that Should be Born". Another reason against the prophetic character of the second section of the book is, it is asserted, that it is addressed to a living people, for how

---

[1] "Bible Investigator" for 1909-1910, to which I acknowledge my indebtedness in preparing this article. "Are there two Isaiahs?" p. 262, by J. Urquhart.

could a man comfort a generation not yet born? But is it inconceivable, for instance, that a dying father should write words of comfort for his posthumous child? God's Word again and again is written for those not yet born. In the prediction of Isaiah 25. 7, that God "will destroy the face of the covering cast over all people, and the veil that is spread over all nations, . . . swallow up death in victory . . . wipe away tears from off all faces" (indeed, one might quote the whole of these chapters), is there no comfort even for ourselves? Does not chapter 40. 2 bring comfort to men not yet born? for truly it cannot yet be said that "the warfare of Jerusalem is accomplished." But believing Israelites may be comforted by the thought that one day it will be so. Another fact that necessitates this theory to the Higher Critical mind is the naming of Cyrus in chapters 44. 28, and 45. 1, for how could a man be named before his birth? But why should this be thought incredible? Cyrus is not the only case in the Bible. Ishmael, Isaac, Solomon, and Josiah (1 Kings 13. 2) are other instances, and John and our Lord Himself in the New Testament. Indeed Josiah was named much longer before his birth than Cyrus in these chapters, if we accept their traditional date.

"Things that are to Come Hereafter". To deny prediction in Isaiah 40. 66 is to be in flagrant contradiction to the Spirit of this section, which is nothing if not predictive. The whole argument of the beginning of the second section of Isaiah, as to the superiority of Jehovah over every rival, rests on His ability to foretell future events. He challenges the idols to do likewise. "Produce your cause, bring forth your strong reasons, saith the King of Jacob; let them bring them forth *and show us what shall happen or declare things to come* . . . Show *the things that are to come hereafter,* that we may know that ye are gods" (chap 41. 21, 23); and then at once occur the words referring no doubt to Cyrus, "I have raised up one from the north, and he shall come."

Then again, in verse 26, Jehovah asks, "Who hath declared from the beginning that we may know?" and after predicting judgment on Babylon, Jehovah (chap 44. 28) names Cyrus as the future deliverer of Israel, and this before promising to open before him the two-leaved gates, etc., and use him for the destruction of Babylon.

Jehovah Challenges all Rivals. "Ask of Me *things to come* concerning My sons, and concerning the work of My hands command ye Me." (Isa 45. 11). And then lastly, in the following chapter, we read: "I am God, and there is none else. I am God, there is none like Me, *declaring the end from the beginning* and from ancient times *the things that are not yet done,* saying, My counsel shall stand, and I will do all my pleasure." Surely no man of honour would claim credit for foresight he did not possess or for discoveries he had never made, and yet the Higher Critics make the writer they call "the Great Unknown" forge (even Cheyne admits them to be professedly prophetic) these documents and make God a party to the fraud, and instead of condemning the whole proceeding they approve. It would be as true to deny colour in a rainbow as prediction in prophecy. If chapter 40 began a prophecy by a new prophet his name would certainly appear at the head of the section according to the invariable custom. The absence of a fresh name shows it is by the same writer who uttered the first part of the prophecy.

The Unity of Authorship of the Book. Another reason for believing in the unity of authorship are the quotations from the second section in prophecies antecedent to the date assigned to it by the Critics. Thus, Jeremiah 31. 35 is a quotation from Isaiah 51. 15: "Which divideth the sea when the waves thereof roar; the Lord of hosts is His name." How could Jeremiah, writing in the reign of Zedekiah, quote from a book written ex-hypothesi after the captivity? Again, how could Zephaniah, writing in the reign of Josiah (that is, in the 7th century B.C.) quote as he does in chapter

2. 15 from Isaiah 47. 8, 10: "That sayest in thine heart, I am, and none else beside me?" The Hebrew word for "beside," *aph-see,* only occurs in these two passages. A third instance is Nahum 1. 15, written a little later than Isaiah, which seems clearly an adaptation of Isaiah 52. 7: "How beautiful upon the mountains are the feet of Him that bringeth good tidings, that publisheth peace." As a matter of fact Isaiah 40 dovetails perfectly into chapter 39. Hezekiah had been consoled by the assurance that the threatened judgment would not be in his day. Were then those who should endure that judgement to be left comfortless? No, they are assured that their judgment will have an end.

Appendix 2

WHO WAS PIERCED?

CONCERNING Zechariah 12. 10, "They shall look on Me whom they pierced" (AV); did the prophet write *eh-lay,* "on Me," or *eh-layv,* "on Him?" In the usual edition of the Hebrew Bible we have the former. The Jewish authorities who made an appendix to the Revised Version in 1896 told us to read, "And they (*i.e.,* the house of David and the inhabitants of Jerusalem) shall look up to me, because of Him, they (*i.e.,* the nations which come against Jerusalem) have pierced."

But this is, as Dr A Lukyn Williams remarks, "A startling translation," for how can "because of Him whom" be got out of *eth asher? Eth* may mark out definitely the following

asher as an object; it cannot be translated "because of."
Besides, does the passage read as though there were a
change of subject here? Must not they who "pierced" be,
according to the natural sequence of thought, the same as
"they who look upon?"

What, then, does the "piercing" mean. It is not enough to
make it mean the suffering of great pain and anguish by
God on account of the sin of His people. Nowhere in
Scripture do we find *dāh-Kar* with this meaning. It always,
as it seems, connotes death (*e.g.*, see chap 13. 8).

Appendix 3

THE RABBIS AND THE MESSIAH

EARLY Jewish interpreters did not contest the Messianic
application of this chapter. In fact Jonathan Ben Uzziel
expressly speaks to this effect in the Chaldee paraphrase; so
the Talmud of Babylon (in Tr. Sanhedrin) applies Isaiah
53. 4 to the Messiah. At the passover, too, they pray,
"Hasten and cause the shadows to flee away. Let Him be
exalted and extolled, and be very high; let Him deal
prudently." It was also assumed as indisputable by the
Christian fathers and universally acknowledged by the Jews
until Aben Ezra, about A.D. 1150, when under the pressure
of controversy the traditional interpretation was
abandoned. Rabbi Solomon Ben Jarchi begins some of his
expositions of the Psalms and prophecies with the following
word of explanation: "This the ancient rabbis understood
of the Messiah, but on account of the use made hereof by

our adversaries it is *more safe* to interpret it of David, Hezekiah," etc. It may be more safe, but is it more true?

Josiah? Jeremiah? or Israel?. It has indeed become the fashion among Jewish teachers in later years to seek an application in Isaiah 53 to Josiah, Jeremiah, or even the whole nation of Israel, instead of to the suffering Messiah, as heretofore, and the rabbis warned by the application of it by Christian writers to Jesus the Messiah have omitted it from the lectionaries, but they still confess, at least once a year, on the Day of Atonement, in the special prayers for the day, that it does refer to Him: "Messiah our righteousness had departed from us. With our wickedness and misdeeds He was burdened, and He was wounded for our transgressions, bearing on the shoulder our sins in order to find an atonement for our iniquities; may we be healed by His wounds!"

Only One Solution. How Josiah could fit in to this chapter is hard to say. He was certainly wounded to death by Pharaoh Necho through interfering in what was in no way his business, but he was honoured by his own people in his life and death. Jeremiah did indeed suffer reproach as a faithful servant of Jehovah, but not voluntarily, silently, or vicariously. Still less does the nation of Israel satisfy the requirements of the chapter. No doubt she has suffered, but to apply to her the idea of one *voluntarily* suffering at the hands of Jehovah, as the *spotless victim* for the sins of others, is altogether far fetched and contrary to the facts. How can Israel possibly fit in with the last words of chapter 52, not to speak of chapter 53, where the clearest distinction is drawn between the Person rejected and His rejecters – the very nation of Israel. How can the "we" and "he" be the same person? How can those who speak of "our transgressions," "our iniquities," "our peace" be the same as the One who was wounded and bruised? No doubt the Jews have suffered at the hands of so-called "Christian nations," acting in a supremely unchristian spirit, but never have they suffered for their persecutors. Some assert that in verse 8 "*neh-gag lamo,*" "was he stricken" (lit., "was the stroke on Him"), ought to be "were they striken," but this is very doubtful. Certainly the word "lamo" is usually plural, but in its first occurrence it is applied separately to Shem and Japheth, though single persons (Gen 9. 26, 27). In both verses "Canaan shall be a servant to him" (lamo). It is certainly also used in the singular in Isaiah 44. 15: "He maketh it a graven image and falleth down *thereto.*" Indeed earlier in his prophecy Isaiah calls Israel a "sinful nation" (chap 1. 4), and she had a large share in inflicting sufferings on the Messiah, who was "despised of the people" (Psa 22. 6).

Divine Relations
before
the Incarnation

Divine Relations before the Incarnation

1

THE CASE STATED

THE Person of Christ occupies such a pre-eminent place in Divine revelation, as to be altogether essential to its completeness and stability. As soon think to alter the sun's place without affecting the equilibrium of the solar system, as to tamper with the Person of Christ without dislocating the whole body of Divine truth.

Not only so, but that Person is a complete entity which cannot be impaired in any respect without the integrity of the whole being compromised. A maimed Christ is not the Christ of God, however much those who derogate from His Person may assure us to the contrary, or indeed believe it to be so.

Nor is it necessary for this, to deny our Lord's eternal pre-existence or essential Deity: Satan has a snare for every circle of believers, and where he knows that mere crude attacks on such truths would be rejected, he has other ways of "casting Him down from His excellency," by denials, for instance, such as those, we have specially in view, of the pre-existence of the Divine Logos, as such, or of His eternal relations in the Godhead, as Son to the Father.

Those who propagate such views have been accused of what is known as Sabellianism. This is a mistake. Sabellius of N. Africa (200 AD) taught that God is essentially Uni-personal, and that what we speak of as three Personal Subsistencies in the Unity of the Godhead, were really only threefold in manifestation; that the same Person, as Father, purposed to save; as Son, accomplished redemption, and, as Holy Spirit, came to lead sinners to Christ. Popular illustrations of the "Three in One" – from the nature of light or the mode of existence of certain substances are essentially Sabellian and should be avoided. Such teaching is of course fundamentally unsound. But the special denials combated here lend themselves more to tritheism. Instead of a past eternity and an Old and a New Testament, full of the relations of three Divine Persons in the Unity of Godhead in intimate relation one to another, as Father, Son and Spirit (and no other possible relation is suggested), we are told to think of three Divine Beings, how related is not revealed, in a cold, colourless, blank eternity as far as Divine affections are concerned. Beings all the replica one of another, and of course without any subordination for mutual purposes, which in their shallow way these errorists declare to be imcompatible, "if words mean anything," a favourite phrase of their school, with the *equality* of the Divine Persons, as they understand the phrase.

Having been called some years ago to engage in this controversy, I sought to meet my opponent by pointing out that, if he took from us the Eternal Sonship, the Eternal Fatherhood must go too. This logical necessity he did not seem ready to admit. Indeed I did not expect him to; as it would have given away his case.

But how solemnly true it is that those who deviate ever so little from the truth, are on a fatal incline; the very thing I warned of, has come true; the denial of the Eternal Fatherhood of God and the relation of the Spirit to the other Persons. But it is surprising that teachers who confessedly know so little, should dogmatize so much. If they are so sure that the familiar relations of Father, Son and Spirit are not revealed before the incarnation, how can they be sure that any relations existed?

It is very easy to affirm that Scripture is silent on such a point, but it presumes a very deep acquaintance with all the depths and breadths of Scripture, which those who know it best would hesistate to claim. We may well be slow to accept such a statement, especially as the Church has practically unanimously held down the ages just the contrary. Surely to thrust aside all God's servants in the past, as though He had only spoken to His people in these last few decades, involves some pretention and self-deception. We should resist with every fibre of our being the theory that God has today set over the Church of God on earth some human Leader to convey His message to His people, and to whom we must humbly bow as to an oracle. This is to deny the indwelling Spirit given to all the saints, and of Whom we read "Ye have an unction from the Holy One and ye know all things" (1 John 2. 20). "Ye need not that any man teach you." (1 John 2. 27). If however we fall under the spell of a man, then what the Scriptures actually say means nothing. All must be read in the light of his official interpretation, and a sad twisting of Scripture is the result. Truly, our Lord's words "Be not ye called Rabbi, for One is your Master (Gk. Teacher) even Christ" (Matt 23. 8) are needed today.

Certainly we are nowhere warned concerning Divine relations, as of "the mystery of Christ"; that they were hidden in God in past ages. Nor are we told anywhere that the relations of Father, Son and Spirit only began at the incarnation. The Father's recognition of the Lord Jesus as His Son at His baptism and on the Holy Mount is certainly a shallow argument for denying the pre-existence of that relation; there was indeed something peculiarly fitting in the One who had ever been in the relation of Son becoming Son of Man. By such arguments the pre-existence of Christ or even His deity might be denied. It is indeed a significant fact that though the denial of the Eternal Sonship[1] does not in the case before us involve the denial of His Deity, yet those we are here seeking to meet, do find themselves in the same camp with Arians, Socinians, Unitarians and such like, all of whom agree in denying the former truth, and it can hardly be questioned that this denial does weaken the defence of His Deity. I remember being invited by one who is now an active propagandist of the error opposed here, to be present at a meeting, where the Deity of Christ was being considered. To my concern I soon discovered that my convener, while professing to uphold the Deity of Christ was cooly taking from us one after another the passages generally taken as proving it. Subsequently light was thrown on the incident by his coming out boldly as a denier of the "Eternal Sonship," so that all the verses that spoke of our Lord as "Son of God" or Son of the Living God, etc., could only refer to the incarnation.

It is commonly asserted by the deniers of this truth that after all it is not a question of real moment, affecting the truth of God to any great extent.

I think this is an untenable position.

We believe the Scriptures are full of testimony to the truth, as we know it, and that the Divine relation so clearly revealed in the New Testament, illumines the whole Old Testament and a past eternity, and immensely augments our knowledge of God and His ways.

If this be an error, we are found false witnesses for Christ, and our whole system of interpretation is a mistake and a delusion. We have embellished the truth by adding our erroneous notions to it. If, on the other hand, such relations of love and fellowship have existed from all

---

[1] It is not very ingenuous to try and cast suspicion on the truth expressed by such a phrase as this, which is only used to avoid a long paraphrase, by saying, "We do not find it in Scripture." The same might be said of such phrases as the fall, substitution, the Trinity.

eternity, can it be a light thing to deny them? It can be nothing less than a shutting out of God's revelation as to the mode of His eternal existence.

The "Eternal Sonship," etc., is a most serious belief to hold if false, it is more serious still to deny if true, as the Divine Being that results from such manipulation is quite different from the Triune God – *eternally the same* – Father, Son and Holy Ghost.

2

WHAT IS AT STAKE?

WHAT is meant by the Eternal Sonship is, not that a Divine Person, in becoming flesh became the Son of God, but that the One we know as the Lord Jesus Christ, had always borne to the First Person of the Godhead, the relation of Son to the Father; that there never was a moment in the past eternity when He was not the Son, and that this relation was as necessary in the mystery of the Godhead as the Divine Existence itself.

As we read in John 1. 1-2, He Who "in the beginning was[1] the Word"; Who "was with (pros – in relation to) God," and so a distinct Person; Who "was God," and therefore a Divine Person, and Who was "in the beginning with (again, pros) God," that is Who was no emanation from, or

---

[1] The verb here employed is not "became," as in v 14. "The Word became flesh," but in contrast, "was" of the indefinite past – implying, as Dean Alford remarks, "existence of an enduring and unlimited state of being contrasting with 'became' in v 3 and especially v 14." Surely such a distinction ought to engage the attention of those denying the Eternal existence of the Logos as such!"

subsequent development in the Godhead, but had always existed in this relation, that One "became flesh," that is "entered into complete manhood, and dwelt among us, and we beheld His glory," etc. And what glory should we expect this to be? Do not the above majestic periods oblige us instinctively to connect it with the moral glory of a past eternity, rather than with His subsequent birth at Bethlehem, glorious though that was in its voluntary abasement? The Lord when down here in incarnation became "the first-born of every creature,"[2] for what other place than the firstborn's could the Creator have in descending into His own creation (Col 1. 15)? In resurrection He became "the first-begotten of the dead" (Rev 1. 5), and that in association with "many brethren"; but the term "Only-Begotten" marks His unique relation to the Father *from* all eternity, to be shared by no one else *to* all eternity, not even by the "many sons" (Heb 2. 10) whom God is bringing to glory, with the Captain of their salvation.

The further reference to the Only-Begotten Son in verse 18, seems to lead to the same conclusion. "No man hath seen God at any time; the Only-Begotten Son, which is in (eis) the bosom of the Father, He hath declared Him." The words "at any time" surely must include Old Testament times, and show that the One, spoken of sometimes as a man, sometimes as an angel or the angel of the Lord, Who frequently appeared in the Theophanies of the Old Testament, declaring God to His people, and Who can be shown to be divine, was the Person, Who even then was in relation to the Father as "the Only-Begotten Son." Alford remarks that "eis" carries on the thought of the "pros" in vv 1 and 2. You can no more force the sense of "into" into the first named, than of "toward" in the latter. Chrysostom, who, as a distinguished Christian teacher and Greek theologian, may be supposed to know the Greek idiom,

---

[2] The exact meaning of the phrase will be discussed later.

points out that the form of the Greek – again, *being* (not becoming) in the bosom of the Father denotes much more than mere position "in the bosom"; but "relationsip and oneness of being," the present participle as in chap. 3. 13, "is used to signify *essential truth* without any particular regard to time." The Son was eternally in the bosom of the Father, the place of infinite nearness and affection. It is a sheer wresting of Scripture to say that "He Who became flesh *became* subsequently the Word," when what is specifically stated is, that He Who was the Word became flesh, and almost a bathos to be informed that this was "a name He acquired among the saints." In fact such an idea is contrary both to the usage of the disciples, there being no recorded instance of such a custom, and to the statement of Christ, "ye call Me Master and Lord, and ye say well, for so I am." (John 13. 13). The Lord did not recognise "the Word" as an appellation they used of Him. Long before John wrote thus of the Word, such a description was attributed by Greek religious writers and others, to a mysterious Person in the Old Testament, distinct from the Divine Being, and yet His equal, and it is this Memra of Word which John adopts as applying to the Lord. This we shall refer to again.

It may seem a small matter to some minds to modify Divine Names, but in reality it is nothing short of tampering with Divine Persons, for the Names of God are His qualities, His character, Himself. To substitute for the majestic "Word," denoting not merely the expression of His purposes, but the very *reason* of those purposes – the glorious Person of the Son, a mere human "name acquired among the saints," is to play fast and loose with Divine realities, and to rob the saints of a Divine revelation. To deny the eternal relations of the Father, Son and Spirit is to deprive the Father of an Eternal and sufficient object of His affections, and of the One Who could alone adequately respond by the Eternal Spirit to those affections.

We cannot afford, as members of Christ's Body to ignore our fellow-members in other ages: – Christian teachers – many of whom sealed their testimony with their blood. God has not left Himself without a witness, nor His true Church in darkness as to the Person of Christ. We believe that He has had His servants in every age, perhaps poorly instructed in assembly truth, but mighty in the Scriptures, along certain lines, and patterns of good works. We will close this paper then with a quotation from one such, who is generally considered to have been not only a true and humble christian, but a sound theologian. He thus writes of the Lord: "Meanwhile being divine, being properly God, He is filial, He is the Son . . . See eg., John 1. 18; 17. 5, 24; Col 1. 13-17; Heb 1. 2, 8; 2. 14-17; 1 John 4. 9. Not only as He is Man, but as He is God, He is so related to the Father, that in divine reality, eternally and necessarily, He is the Son; as such, truly possessing the whole nature of "His own Father" (John 5. 18). The inscrutable mode of this blessed Filiation is named in the theology of the Christian Church "the Eternal Generation" . . . Scripture reveals that the Christ is the Son antecedent to incarnation. It also reveals that He is eternal . . . "The Christ did not *become*, but necessarily and eternally *is* the Son". Such has been the general faith of the elect in all ages.

3

HOW THIS QUESTION HAS BEEN RAISED

IT would have been preferable to the present writer in some ways, to leave out all personal references, but now it is proposed to follow apostolic example, and name some who are propagating the denial of the Eternal Sonship, among saints, who are led astray, little suspecting how this "new light" detracts from the glory of the Triune God, and obscures Divine relations in the Old Testament.

The late Mr F E Raven, in a Bible-reading in the USA, put forward the teaching that the Lord's Sonship dated from His incarnation, and that nothing is revealed of any such relations in the Godhead, before that, as Father, Son and Spirit. Such teaching, though not unknown among individuals here and there in the past history of the Church had never, except in the case of Unitarian connexions, formed part of the confession of faith of any church as such. It was moreover in direct opposition to the teaching of those known as "brethren" from the first, and indeed of Mr Raven himself. *This item was accordingly cut out of the published report.* But the seed had fallen into favourable soil, *i.e.*, the mind of Mr Taylor, where however it was allowed to lie quiescent for twenty-five years, while half a generation of "Ravenites" were passing away, innocently singing the praises of the Eternal Son from an unrevised hymn-book, without suspecting the error (!) they were in.

At last, however, in 1929, at a Conference at Barnet, the phychological moment arrived for disseminating the new teaching, as "the spirital condition of the saints was supposed to warrant it." Another reason has been suggested, and one that saddens those who have a heart for the saints and the truth of God. A foundation principle of what is known as the "brethren movement," had been from the first, the continual presence and ministry of the Holy Spirit indwelling the saints, individually and collectively, as their sufficent guide and teacher through the Word, and the direct responsibility of each and all to hear and obey His voice. Sad to say this principle has been largely ousted by a new and contrary principle, namely subservience to one man as a kind of official mouth-piece of that Spirit. A movement that began as a protest against human pretentions has ended in subservience to human dictatorship. The circle has completed itself. To the dismay and grief of a faithful minority, the whole "Ravenite" circle executed a right-about face, and new converts like Mr C A Coates, so widely esteemed hitherto for his written ministry, were found contraverting with some little heat, brethren who were only seeking to defend the truth, he and others had held as vital.

As for the grounds for such a change, we are persuaded that as good and solid arguments could be adduced for accepting Arianism or denying the Deity of the Spirit. We are told that, "the words, Eternal Sonship are not found in Scripture." Arius might ask us to show in Scriputre, in so many words the Son's "Eternal pre-existence," or His essential deity or His co-substantiality[1] with the Father. I can imagine some of these brethren holding up such a phrase as this last to contempt and derision, and yet it was this very phrase which was used of God finally to defeat the deadly system of Arius, which under guise of caressing Christianity was surely strangling it. Could Arius come to life today with his plausible manners and seductive teachings, he would, to judge from recent happenings, make short work of some who profess to be deeply taught in God's truth.

At a conference in Birmingham, Mr J Taylor is reported

---

[1] "Homoousia" instead of the "homoiousia" of Arius.

to have said that though we read of the Spirit being sent from heaven, nowhere is this said of Christ: the idea of being sent involving inferiority. We could only then deduce from this that the Spirit must be an inferior Person of the Godhead, which is Arianism and fundamental heresy. We deny both premises, that being sent necessarily involves inferiority, and that the Lord is never said to be sent from heaven. Peter and John were sent by their fellow-apostles at Jerusalem (Acts 8. 14); Paul and Barnabas from Antioch (chap 11. 30), not as inferiors, but because specially suitable for the service in hand. The Lord Jesus says Himself "I came down from heaven, not to do mine own will, but the will of *Him that sent Me*" (John 6. 38), where the conclusion seems inevitable that the coming down and the sending were equally from heaven. This involes not inferiority but subordination to common ends, with which agree the words "My Father *giveth you* the true bread from (out of) heaven." (John 6. 32). If sending a Person involved inferiority in the sent one, giving Him would equally. We read again and again of God sending His Son into the world. "Say ye of Him whom the Father hath sanctified and sent into the world, Thou blasphemest because I said unto you, I am the Son of God?" (John 10. 36). Now we know the Lord was "foreordained before the foundation of the world" (1 Peter 1. 20). Would it not be very arbitrary to dissociate His being "set apart" for this eternal purpose, from His being sent into the world? or to maintain that though the former divine operation took place in the heavenly sphere, the sending into the world must be limited to the earthly – namely that of the incarnation? It reads more naturally to take them together. Let us not "put asunder, what God has joined together." (Mark 10. 9). For mark, it was the Father who sanctified and sent Him, so that He was the Son when sanctified as well as when sent.

It is true that the Lord compares the apostles' mission with His own, "As Thou hast sent me into the world, even so have I also sent them into the world" (John 17. 18), and much is made by these teachers of this comparison. But if the emphasis is on the "whither" of the mission, rather than on the fact of the mission, the comparison breaks down, for *ex hypothesi* the incarnation was the great crisis for the Lord. It was then He was sent, whereas it was not at birth that the apostles were sent. As a matter of fact "world" has the two senses in Greek, as with us, of a geographical locality, and a moral sphere. The Lord was sent from heaven to earth as the former, as well as to the latter, not to do His own will, but the *Father's,* so it was as the *Son* He came, for "in the volume[2] of the book" it was written of Him, "Lo I come to do Thy will, O God." (Heb 10. 7). In any case it is not legitimate to force a comparison to cover all the points in the two terms. During the last War the King may have sent the Prince of Wales to the front from Buckingham Palace and he as Colonel of the Welsh Guards may have sent them, using some phrase analogous to the words we are considering, "As the King, my father, has sent me to the front, so I send you," but without prejudice to the fact that his mission started from the Palace; theirs from their barracks. So the Lord's mission started from heaven, and theirs from Galilee, but their destination was the same – the world. Again we read in Gal 4. 4., "God *sent* forth His Son, made of a woman, made under law." The word *sent* is the same full word (exapostello: send away out of) as in verse 6 of the sending of the Spirit. Surely the sending forth in both cases is from the same heavenly sphere. "He sent forth His Son": was it from heaven or from Bethlehem? – the following phrase replies the former – for he was both made of a woman: – His birth as man, and made under law: – His birth as a Jew, *after being sent.* The order is divine and to tamper with it is a solemn responsibility – sent forth as Son,

---

[2] This "volume" cannot well be the Old Testament, for the words occur in Psalm 40. It is rather, we would suggest, the book of God's Eternal Counsels.

born at Bethlehem, circumcized the eighth day. This is the true order. The same is clear in Heb 1. 2, to him that hath ears to hear: "God in these last days hath spoken unto us by His Son, Whom He hath appointed heir of all things, by Whom also He made the worlds." Now we never speak of an "heir and son" being born, but of "a son and heir." So the Lord was Son before He was heir, and heir before creation, for that followed, to provide the inheritance. The truth is dislocated, if we reverse the order.

Of course there are cases where it is permissible to refer to a person by a name subsequently acquired, that is when there is no ambiguity. Thus a man might say "I met my wife"; meaning the one who subsequently became his wife. But the phrase does not lose its ordinary meaning, because of this exceptional use. Pharaoh's daughter never said we may be sure, "I found my son in an ark of bulrushes," meaning I found a babe who afterwards became my son; yet this is what Son is always forced to mean by these new teachers. To attach to the frequent phrases "God gave His only begotten Son," "God sent His only Son," etc., the meaning of one who subsequently became His Son, is arbitrarily to make of an exceptional use, the rule, and has the appearance at least of reversing the Word of God in the most unjustifiable way.

4

SOME FALLACIES EXPOSED

THE sublime sentences at the beginning of John's Gospel, to recur to them once more, have always been understood by Christian teachers to be an unequivocal revelation of the reality and character of Divine relations in a past Eternity. Presentday deniers of any such revelation ask us to substitute in each of the nine occurrences of "the Word" (Gk. Logos), expressed or understood, in John 1, 1-14, the periphrasis "the One who afterwards acquired this name among the saints." Such a request puts too great a strain on the spiritual intelligence of most saints. There is no tangible proof that the Lord Jesus ever did acquire such a name among the saints; we certainly never heard Him addressed as such. Such an idea must have been invented for the occasion. The only possible instance is a doubtful one in Luke 1. 2, without serious authority[1]. It rests primarily on a mistaken meaning assigned to "The Word," as the "One Who spoke God's word," or "Who was the word spoken," either of which meanings as Dr Alford shows, would be otherwise represented in the Greek. The "Logos" means rather God's "Reason" for all His purposes – the One in Whom they all centre. If this be so, could a greater bathos be conceived than the suggested reversal?[2] Mr C A Coates, however, tries to justify it with Scriptural examples. He cites Exodus 6. 3 and Ephesians 1. 3. Let us see what these really mean. In the first the Lord says, "I am Jehovah, and I appeared unto Abraham, unto Isaac, and unto Jacob by the name of God Almighty, but by my name Jehovah was I not

---

[1] These teachers would set on one side, as out of date, Mr J N Darby, who certainly was by grace a giant doctrinally, because he held fast the "Eternal Sonship," and as though we could have "new light" from God's Spirit to reverse foundation truths. But in a matter of Greek scholarship, on which, if for no other reason, he had not time to be equally schooled, they magnify his authority to assert that in Luke 1. 2 "word" ought to be "Word". If so the mass of Christian teachers, commentators, Versions, English and foreign, are wrong. The present writer only has Darby's French Version, and that gives "word" in the text and in a footnote, "or Word." And this was, as we know, his original version.

[2] The Bible of these beloved brethren ought almost to be called "The Reversed Version."

known to them." Mr Coates points out what has often been noticed, that the name Jehovah does occur frequently in Genesis and not least in connection with the patriarchs. To explain this apparent discrepancy, he asserts that Moses must have written Genesis, after the Divine declaration, in Exodus 6, (which is doubtful), and that in every previous occurrence of the name "Jehovah," we must understand their favourite turn of phrase – "the one afterwards known as Johovah." But by what right could Moses make such a change or for what object? seeing the Divine names "God," "Most High," "Almighty God," were more suited to the epoch? It is an impossible explanation, seeing it would involve changing the very words of God, *e.g.,* to Jacob – "I am Jehovah God of Abraham" (Gen 28. 13). What does Mr Coates suppose this was originally? or the direct words of Jacob – "Then shall Jehovah be my God" (v 21), or the plain statement concerning Isaac – "He called upon the name of Jehovah" (chap 26. 25). And by what name did Abraham call the Mount, if not "Jehovah-Jireh?" (chap 22. 14). The whole theory is fantastical. There is a simple explanation. God does not say that the name Jehovah was not known, but that *He was not known* in that name, that is the patriarchs did not yet know its divine meaning. To illustrate further Israel knew well the name of Father (see Isa 63. 16; Jer 31. 9; Matt. 1. 17), but not God as Father. Many know the name of Jesus, who do not know the Lord Jesus!

The second verse is equally inconclusive. "The God and Father of our Lord Jesus Christ" had just been mentioned as the Blesser of His people. Mr Coates argues that when it is added "Who chose us," we must understand "the One Whom we know as above." Perfectly right, none would dispute it; but this is the reverse of what Mr Coates wants to prove. We can always go backwards and speak of our Lord Jesus as "the One who was with God in the beginning," etc., but we nowhere read "In the beginning was Jesus";

meaning the One who acquired the name subsequently at His birth.

It is perfectly right of course to find in Gen 1. 2 "The Spirit of God moved upon the face of the waters," because He, "the Eternal Spirit," was existing then as such, but to find the name of "Jesus" in that chapter would be quite out of place. I remember in a discussion some years ago with one of these men, who denied, as is the case today, that even the Holy Spirit had been revealed before the incarnation, pointing out to him the above reference to the Spirit as proving the opposite. He at once replied "That could not be the Holy Spirit"; "And why not, pray?" I asked: "Because He was not then revealed" (!) To such a point can prejudice blind the eyes!

5

OBJECTIONS CONSIDERED

OBJECTIONS to eternal relations, as usually understood, in the Godhead, are based on philosophic difficulties, rather than on the Scriptures. Inferences are drawn from our human use of the words "Generation," "Fatherhood," "Sonship," and analogies are treated as identities. But this we must carefully avoid, as we do instinctively, when we speak of Christ as the Head of the Body, or as the Bridegroom of the Church. Certainly there are difficulties, but how expect to understand the Being of God, when we do not even understand our own? If we could explain Divine Relations, either they would cease to be Divine, or we should be so. It is "by" faith we understand." (Heb 11.

2). But no, everything must be made intelligible; there must be no mysteries. Heresies are usually intellectual efforts by self-sufficient persons to explain Divine Truth. If anything, they explain it away. The Monophysite heresy was to explain the difficulty of the two natures in One Person; the Monothelite, that of the two wills in One Person; Nestorianism the difficulty of One Person in two natures. Any Sunday School scholar could grasp the Arian "Trinity" – God created the Son: the Son created the Spirit. But the Scriptural doctrine of the Triune God transcends man's highest thought; and so with the truth of Divine Relations. Any natural man can apprehend the human modern theory, here combated: – "God *became* the Father of Jesus at Bethlehem, and He the Son." But, as a fact, the Father is never mentioned as the Agent of the Incarnation, but always and only the Holy Spirit. Thus, "She was found with Child of the Holy Ghost"; "That which is conceived (Gk. begotten) in her is of the Holy Ghost." "The Holy Ghost shall come upon thee" (Matt 1. 18, 20; Luke 1. 35), and yet the Lord is never spoken of as the Son of the Spirit.

Still Zophar's question challenges the "explainers," "Canst thou by searching find out God? Canst thou find out the Almighty unto perfection?" (Job 11. 7). "No man knoweth the Son, but the Father; neither knoweth any man the Father save the Son, and he to whomsoever the Son will reveal Him" (Matt 11. 27). It is not equally the Father's will to explain the complex Person of the Son, as it is the Son's to reveal the Father. But a son does not know his father by the fact of human birth. And how can this unique mutual knowledge, existing between the Father and the Son, depend on or originate in the Incarnation?

But some who admit the Eternal Fatherhood and Sonship are deceived by the reasoning of Arius "If the Father begat the Son, He who was begotten had a beginning of existence, so there was a time when the Son did not exist." But would an arch-heretic like Arius be capable of correct inferences from Divine truth? However we are asked in face of what one writer calls "the inexorable logic of Arius" to revise the meaning of "Only-begotten," to signify merely "Beloved." But the Greek word – monogenés, is translated in all its nine occurrences in the New Testament "only begotten" or its equivalent; five times of our Lord (John 1. 14, 18; 3. 16, 18, and 1 John 4. 9); and of only children in Luke 7. 12; 8. 42; 9. 38, and Heb 11. 17. Though in the last passage Isaac had a brother Ishmael, Genesis 22. 2 makes it plain that God did not reckon him, the brother after the flesh, as a true son of Abraham. AV and RV are at one in maintaining "only begotten," and with them agree most with any claim to be authorities.[1]

If people say they do not understand, it only proves in fact that they do not understand. Perhaps some day we will. In the meantime what God has clearly revealed persists in spite of our nescience.

As one has well said, "The relation which . . . has always subsisted and actually subsists in the Godhead between the Father and the Son – whatever may be its precise nature . . . is that which truly and properly constitutes Sonship, and is the original idea or archetype of filiation." And again "we ought to regulate our conceptions of what sonship is and implies, not from the defective and imperfect human relations, but from the original and only true idea of it as subsisting between the First and Second Persons of the Godhead." In other words we must not argue from the human to the Divine, but from the Divine to the human.

Another fallacy underlies the above argument of Arius,

---

[1] Grimm does not recognise the possibility of such a change. Alford is dead against it. Ellicott says "the sense is fixed as" the eternal generation of the Word, "the only-begotten Son of God, begotton of the Father before all worlds." J N Darby translates in his French version, "fils unique," which is the French equivalent for "only Son."

and of those whose epouse his logic. It is of attaching time to Divine Relations; in fact, of confusing time and its concomitant ideas of "beginning," "priority," "subsequence," etc., with eternity, in which these cannot subsist.

As another has said "Let the notion of time come into the conception given of God-head, and of the Persons – Father, Son and Holy Ghost and all would be falsehood and confusion" and higher: "The Son of God never was made the Son. He is never even called the child (teknon) of God." Surely the fact should give pause to those who connect Sonship with the Lord's human birth. Even the new-birth does not in the strict sense constitute a beliver a son, but a child of God. At His birth our Lord was not born, but given as a Son (see Isa 9. 6). To be thus given He must have been Son before the virgin birth. For when God calls by a Name, the reality is there first. So that in this passage we read of that Son, "His name shall be called, Wonderful, Counsellor, the Mighty God," etc. He did not become thse for the first time then. Likewise in Luke 1. 35 "That Holy Thing which shall be born of thee, shall be *called* the Son of God," because He was it before. The same is true of the name "Jesus" (Jehovah is Salvation) for the name of Saviour already belonged to Jehovah (Isa 45. 21).

6

PERSONAL DIFFERENCES IN THE GODHEAD

THE denial of any relevation in the Old Testament concerning Divine Relations[1] or of the retrospective character of much revealed in the New, is a claim to know exhaustively the whole range of revelation. "And if any man think that he knoweth anything (*i.e.,* exhaustively) he knoweth nothing yet as he ought to know." (1 Cor 8. 2). The result is the veiling for all time of the Divine glory, up to the incarnation; and, more serious even than that, a tampering with the true character of the Divine mode of existence, because in order as they think, to safeguard the equality of Divine Persons, which we too, firmly hold, they describe them as identical in every respect in a condition of "Absolute Deity" and deny all relations of subordination between them. The result is "tritheism," as has already been pointed out; and a Unitarian might object – "Why should three Divine Persons, all infinite, eternal, omnipotent, be needed, and One not suffice? This would be sound reasoning were the Persons such as these teachers depict them. But what does the expression that is met with in these writers, "absolulte Deity" mean? Is not the Deity of the Father, Son and Spirit absolute? or are there two kinds of Deity? Did the incarnation deprive Divine Persons of "absolute Deity?" The unchangeableness of God is insisted on again and again in the Scriptures: "I am the Lord, I change not." (Mal 3. 6). "With Whom is no variableness neither shadow of turning." (Jas 1. 17). But if these teachers

---

[1] A tardy admission is made that relations of love and glory must have existed, in the Godhead, but not a revelation of such.

were right, God would have changed, would have proved variable. His Deity is not now, what it once was – absolute! There is, of course, not a scintilla of proof of such an unsound and dangerous theory. But this *ficticious* equality did not exist even between Jehovah and the Angel of the Covenant, or between Jehovah and the One whom He calls His Spirit. The root error of all this defective "theology"[2] is the failure to recognize the functional differences between the Persons of the Trinity. "There is but one God, the Father," (1 Cor 8. 6). To Him belongs origination: – "of whom are all things, and we in Him": election "according to His own foreknowledge" "and times or seasons" (Acts 1. 7), etc. How is it conceivable that, if "all things are of the Father," He did not exist as such before all things, and *a fortiori* before the incarnation? How else could He choose His people, or have foreknowledge of them? And yet we are blandly told, "Scripture does not say so." But Scripture does say so, unless it be twisted out of all recognition. It is an echo of the "Hath God said?" (Gen 3. 1) of Eden, and the same "twister" of God's word is, it is to be sadly feared, behind both twistings.

To resume, to the Son belongs execution and administration "by whom are all things and we in Him," (1 Cor 8. 6). He carries out the Divine purposes; He is the agent in Creation and Redemption. He does not send or give the Father, but the Father Him, and that "from heaven." To this the Lord bears clear testimony: "The bread of God is He which *cometh down from heaven* and giveth life unto the world" (John 6. 33). *"My Father giveth you* the true bread from heaven" (v. 32) *"I came down from heaven,* not to do mine own will, but with the will of Him

---

[2] "Theology," which these teachers profess to hold in such disrepute, though indulging in it when it seems convenient, is only an orderly apprehension of what it has pleased God to reveal in His word. John was a theologian, for "John the divine" is only "John the theologian" (theologos): – of course every teacher must be more or less a theologian.

that sent me." (John 6. 38). This Scripture clearly affirms that the coming and the sending were both from heaven. The Lord came because He was sent. *"I came forth from the Father and am come in to the world; again I leave the world* and go to the Father" (John 16. 28). I should have thought it clear that the "leaving the world" in the second part of this verse describes the ascension, marking the return journey to the very point from whence the coming forth from the Father started. Therefore our Lord did come forth from the Father, and knew Him in that relation before the incarnation. One more verse may suffice: – "And now, O Father, glorify thou me with Thine own self with the glory, which I had with Thee, before the world was" (John 17. 5). By what feat of religious *legerdemain* the above verses can be made to harmonize with this sad denial of the Eternal relations of the Father and the Son, I do not profess to understand. I am afraid the only thing to say is with the Apostle Paul, "Let God be true but every man (even though he come to us with the highest claims to spiritual intelligence) a liar"! (Rom 3. 4). They say they "shrink from going a hair-breadth beyond what Scripture says," but ought we not equally to shrink from stopping a hair-breadth short of what Scripture says? To take away, is as serious as to add.

To recur to our thesis, the Holy Spirit, thought co-equal with the Father and the Son, was sent forth by them (John 14. 26; 16. 7). One of these teachers, as we have seen, affirmed that it would be derogatory for a Divine Person to be sent by another;and therefore our Lord could only have been sent after Incarnation, but if this were so, it would deny the Deity both of the Lord Jesus and, as we have seen, of the Spirit, and land us in Arianism right away. It is by His power that the Divine purposes are fulfilled; by Him – the Eternal Spirit – "Christ offered Himself without spot to God." (Heb 9. 14). He convicts, converts, sanctifies, reveals Christ and things to come. The Spirit is named throughout the Old Testament from Genesis to Malachi as "the Spirit," "the Spirit of God," "My Spirit" (*e.g.,* Gen 1. 2; 6. 3; Ezek 11. 24; Zech 4. 6) and is clearly the One and only Divine Spirit of Scripture. To talk about "inscrutability" to nullify all this, is to throw dust in the saints' eyes. "Those things which are revealed belong unto us and to our children." (Deut 29. 29). We do know the "Only true God and Jesus Christ whom Thou hast sent," (John 17. 3) etc., etc. "Inscrutability" can only mean that we cannot know Him, apart from, and beyond His Self-revelation.

7

PROOFS FROM THE OLD TESTAMENT

MUST we then admit that nothing is revealed of Divine relations in the Old Testament Scriptures? We cannot, with those Scriptures in our hands. It may, of course, be premised, that we do not expect in the Old Testament a *full* revelation of this any more than of other truths, but we have the foreshadowings, as well as the retrospective revelation of the New. The truth is "patent in the New, latent in the Old"; "The New unfolds, what the Old enfolds."

Certainly the great truth of the Old Testament is the Unity of the Godhead, in contrast with the polytheistic idolatory, into which man had fallen. But the first verse of Genesis reveals that the Unity of the Godhead does not preclude a plurality of Persons in the Godhead, and this is manifest, as we proceed, both in the theophanies and in the direct teaching of Scripture. This is admitted by all who hold Trinitarian truth. But we go further; we find definite indications in the Old Testament that the relations described in the New Testament, as those of Father and Son, already existed. Let us turn, for instance, to Psalm 2. No doubt this is mainly prophetic to the end of verse 9, but as is frequent in prophecy, we come in the last three verses to truth of present application, introduced as it is in the Hebrew text by the words "And *now.*" This was an actual appeal (no doubt true in all time also) to Kings whom David had primarily in view. "And *now* be wise, oh ye kings . . . serve Jehovah with fear . . . Kiss the Son, lest he be angry . . . blessed are all they that put their trust in Him." Who then is this Son? Although the word (bar) is not the usual one, its only other occurrence being Prov 31. 2, yet it is frequently used in names such as Bar-jonah, Barnabas, Barsabas, Bar-Jesus. Here the Son is mentioned side by side with Jehovah as His equal, the final arbiter of man's destinies – the suffcent object of his trust, clearly therefore a Divine Person. How rash then to affirm that such relations as Father and Son (in the Godhead) are quite foreign to the Old Testament. It is to deny the force of plain expressions used by the Spirit Himself.

One word of God outweighs all other words. "Every word of God is pure." (Prov 30. 5). It is noteworthy that the passage which preceeds these words bears explicit witness to Sonship in the Godhead. We have here the remarkable seven-fold question of Agur as to Creation and then as to the names of Creator and His Son. "What is His name, and *what is His Son's name if thou canst tell?*" (Prov 30. 4). This is evaded in the usual way, it is prophetical. Are we not told as much? Well at any rate it is not a prophecy that the Creator should have a Son: that is taken for granted, but as to that Son's name. There is nothing really prophetical in the passage. As a matter of fact the word translated here "prophecy," is only so translated in one other of its 70 ocurrences in the Old Testament, and that is in the following chapter 31. 1, "the prophecy that his mother taught him," where again there is nothing prophetical in the whole context, but rather a weighty warning against vice and strong drink. The root meaning is really "a burden" or something of weight. Gesenius translates in Prov. 31 1, "sentences": the Revised Version in both places "burden" or "oracle." It is what we would call a "weighty statement." Surely to affirm then that Sonship in the Godhead is unknown in the Old Testament is to deny what is plainly written. Agur had no pretention, as he tells us himself, to be highly educated or gifted or deeply taught in divine truth, but he knew more than some who make these claims today, and yet have let go what he knew. May the Lord give us more Agurs, simple men who hold the truth tenaciously, and enquire for more!

This agrees too with what devout students of the Word have learnt of the Divine Wisdom (Prov 8). This has been held from time immemorial by Christian and Jewish interpreters, as revealing a mysterious plurality in the Divine Being. But these men brush it all on one side, on some tiny pretext which *proves* their point, as they assert. One wonders at their facile logic[1]. Only those already persuaded could attach weight to it. How could a mere attribute, reprove, demand obedience, counsel, rejoice before God, be sinned against? How strikingly reminiscent of the statements of John 1. are such words as, "The Lord possessed me in the beginning of His way before His works of old." "I was set up from everlasting or ever the earth was." "When there were no depths I was brought forth!" (vv

[1] The whole argument from Prov. 8. is waived aside in oracular fashion. "It must be admitted by all (!) that the thought of Son is simply not to be found there, wisdom being personified as a woman" (C A Coates Remarks p. 45). This is only because wisdom is feminine in Hebrew, as in Greek. By the same shewing any Frenchman could prove that the Word in John 1. 3 is "personified as a woman" – as the word "Parole" is feminine and the pronouns are feminine. The same is true of Light in v 8 – it must be a woman, because the word is feminine in French. We have seen that the thought of Son is anything but foreign to such an

22 to 25). Here we have twice the thought of "generation" – "I was brought forth," "I was brought forth" (Heb. chul. see Job 15. 7, "Wast thou *made* before the hills?" Psa 51. 5, *"shapen* in iniquity"). How can we avoid the conclusion that it is the Eternal Son who was then brought forth? Clearly eternal filiation and eternal existence in the past are not incompatible, however much human reason may stumble.

The truth is further illustrated by the familiar words of Micah 5. 2, "Out of thee (Bethlehem) shall He *come forth* unto Me, that is to be ruler in Israel; Whose *goings forth* have been from of old from everlasting." The first phrase without controversy foretells the human birth, but the same root *yat-tzah* is used of "the goings forth from everlasting." The word is used frequently for birth (e.g., Gen 25. 26; Exod 21. 22; Job 1. 21; 3. 11; 38. 29). It seems difficult to believe that the Holy Spirit can have used the same word in juxta-position, unless He had wished to emphasize the fact that the One born in Bethlehem, had already existed in the eternal past as the Divine Son. This exactly harmonizes with the expression in Isa 9. 6, "Unto us a child is born, unto us a Son is *given*." – the very One who had been from the beginning, the Word, the Eternal Son of God.

---

expression as "I was brought forth" (vv 24 and 25). To this Mr. J. Taylor himself once bore unswerving testimony. In a book entitled "Resurrection and Levitical Privilege" (1911). Referring to this very passage far from admitting what Coates asserts, he writes, "The expression 'Brought up with Him,' 'daily His delight,' that was not Adam that was 'THE SON.'" What is there to show that Mr. Taylor was not taught of God, when he held this view? Evidently he attached no importance to the shallow reasoning which to Coates is now determinant.

8

THE THEOPHANIES

ONE of the essential attributes of God is His Invisibility; He is *aoratos:* (Col 1. 15; 1 Tim 1. 17, etc.). This, when applied to Him in His Essence must mean, not only that He cannot, but may not be seen; "Whom no man hath seen, nor can see" (1 Tim 6. 16). Not even Moses could have looked on the face of God and lived. If God is to reveal Himself to the creature, it must be by an interpreting medium.

Who then could fulfil this function of Intermediary? The truth of John 1. 18 is of the first importance in replying to this question. Let us note once more its terms; "No man (Greek: 'no one') hath seen God AT ANY TIME; the only Begotten Son, which is in[1] the bosom of the Father, He hath declared him." Which is (in the bosom) is lit.: "the One being," not "becoming" as it would have been had it been a relation begun in time. The phrase denotes, not mere position, but relationship and oneness of being, essential truth without any particular regard to time. He knows and declares as none other could. This was true before the worlds were made. As we do not see the Sun itself, but its effulgence, so no angel ever saw God, except through the Son, who was "the brightness (lit. 'reflected brightness') of His glory" (Heb 1. 3). This was also true in Old Testament times. The appearances of God to Abraham, Moses, Joshua, etc., usually called "Theophanies," ought rather to be called

---

[1] The preposition "eis," here translated "in," has usually, but not always, the sense of "into"; but it does not alter the truth of the verse whichever it is here.

[2] From two words "huios" (a Son) and "phaino" (to appear).

"Huiophanies,"[2] for none but the only begotten Son could have declared Him even then; and such has been the belief of the Church from the beginning, based on the explicit statement of John 1. 18. How great the dishonour done to the Glorious Person of the Son of God, that this, His peculiar prerogative, as Revealer of God, should be snatched from Him! Truly the present-day denial that we are seeking to combat here, is (unknown to its authors) only one more Satanic attempt to "cast Him down from His Excellency!" (Psa 62. 4).

We will now briefly consider some of these appearances . . . It is true that the one who appears is often called "the Angel of the Lord," "Angel of the Covenant," or simply "Angel," but the Hebrew "malach" has, like its Greek equivalent, the double sense of angel and messenger. Jacob uses the word in his review of God's dealings. "The Angel which redeemed me from all evil, bless the lads" (Gen 48. 16). This would undoubtedly include the incidents of Bethel (Gen 28. 13), of Haran (31. 10), of Peniel (32. 35), of Beersheba (41. 1). Would the patriarch at such a moment call on a mere angel to bless his grandsons. None but the Son of God could redeem? Stephen speaks of the "Angel of the Lord," who appeared to Moses out of the midst of a bush. But in Exodus 3. that very angel becomes, a moment later, God Himself, affirming, "I am the God of Abraham," (v 6) etc. Certainly a mere angel could not render the place too holy for Moses to stand on with unshodden feet, or be too much for his eyes to look on. That would be to give the glory of God to another. The "brightness of His glory," which the Son was, was seen in the Shekinah Glory, and in the pillar of fire. It is true that angels had their subordinate share in the events of Sinai, but no one can read Exodus 11. and doubt who was the ultimate Lawgiver. Exodus 19. 3, 5, and 20 settle the matter. "All the earth is mine" (v 5). "God spake all these words" (20. 1). And then we read in chapter 24: "They saw the God of Israel," (v 10) it was no similitude that they beheld, but the glory of "the only-begotten Son."

The same august Person must be referred to in Exodus 23, 20, "Behold I send an Angel before thee," for no one but a Divine Person can "pardon trangressions," or have God's name in Him. Also in Joshua 5. 14, the "Captain of the host of the Lord," before whom the lesser captain took off his shoes and worshipped, was none other than Jehovah Himself, again revealed in the Son. He was the Mediator, and there is only One.

Further examples might be cited in the lives of Hagar, Balaam, Gideon, and from the prophecy of Zechariah, but one more may suffice – the Angel that appeared to Manoah and his wife (Judges 13. 3). None but the Son of God would have dared to identify himself with the burnt offering, by ascending in its smoke and savour to God? This name "Secret" (pahlah) (v 18) identifies Him with the Son, who should be called "Wonderful" (pahlah) (Isa 9. 6). It is a serious error, as John found, to mistake an angel for the Lord (Rev 19. 10; 20. 9); but much more to mistake the Son of God for an angel! But the proof would be strengthened could a passage be found explicitly identifying the "Angel of the Covenant" with "the Lord Jesus." We find such in Malachi 3. 1, "Behold I will send my Messenger (John the Baptist) and he shall prepare the way before Me, and the Lord, whom ye seek, shall suddenly come to his temple, even the Messenger of the Covenant, whom ye delight in; behold, He shall come, saith the Lord of hosts." Clearly the Lord here spoken of as "the Messenger (or Angel – Malach) of the covenant," whom we have seen to be the Revealer of God throughout the Old Testament, and therefore "the only-begotten Son" of John 1. 18, is none other than the Lord Jesus. How then can it be denied that He was Son before the Incarnation. In the New Testament the Revelation becomes clearer. In the Old Testament we catch glimpses of a living stream in the distance reflecting the glory of the sun; now it passes in full flood with golden waves, but it is the same river. God is revealing Himself in a new and fuller way. "The brightness of His glory" is now focussed in "the express image of His Person."

Theophany gives place to Incarnation. Can there be a doubt through whom this supreme revelation is to be made? God had already prepared His Revealer, "When the fulness of the time was come, God sent forth His SON, made of a woman, made under the Law to redeem them that were under the Law, that we might receive the adoption of sons." (Gal 4. 4, 5). Here we have four things in their true moral and historical order; first a Divine relationship previously enjoyed: – "His Son"; then a human condition entered upon; "made of a woman"; a particular connection with the chosen nation – "made under the Law," and a twofold result – redemption and adoption.

9

"THIS DAY HAVE I BEGOTTEN THEE" (PSALM 2. 7).

BEFORE leaving the Old Testament we will consider the above words from the second Psalm, a psalm already referred to in the last paper. This sentence is taken for granted by the new teaching to refer prophetically to the Lord's birth at Bethlehem. But this is not at all the subject of the Psalm, which starts, as Acts 4. 2 shews, with the Lord's final rejection, by Jew and Gentile. The fact that these words are thrice quoted in the New Testament ought to simplify the discovery of their reference, for if in any of the three places the context rules out the Lord's human birth, then it seems clear that another meaning must be sought in the other occurrences. The words in their original setting form part of Jehovah's reply to His enemies. It was not likely that at such a moment He should refer to the incarnation. The importance of that in its place cannot be over estimated, as we have seen; it is fundamental. The virgin birth was the greatest sign ever wrought in the earth till then. Apart from it Jesus could not be the seed of the woman, bruiser of the serpent's head, nor the seed of Abraham, heir to the promises, nor the Son of David, heir to the throne of Israel, nor the sinless Saviour of men. Nor was His humanity docetic, that is only in appearance. Nothing was lacking which constitutes real and complete humanity, spirit, soul and body, otherwise the Atonement was vitiated to the core. But like foundations generally, though prominent at first, and never losing their essentiality, this foundation truth faded from view and was never referred to specifically after the event. It had served its purpose. A fresh sign is introduced after the crucifixion – the resurrection, and this seems undoubtedly the reference. Not that the words "Thou art my Son," etc., apply directly to resurrection but it is to the risen Christ that God bears witness as His eternally Begotten Son.

The three quotations of the words are in Acts 13. 33; Heb 1. 5, and 5. 5.

In the last-named passage the subject is Christ's call to priesthood. This could not be by the fact of incarnation, seeing He was of the tribe of Judah. He must first ascend on to a higher plane, where He becomes priest of another order than that of Aaron: – "Thou art a priest forever after the order of Melchizedek." This is quoted from Psa 110. 4 – a Davidic Psalm from which our Lord argues the superiority of David's son – the Messiah, to David from the fact that David acknowledges Him as Lord – a truth explained in Rom 1. 3-4, "Made of the seed of David according to the flesh, and *declared* to be the Son of God with power, according to the Spirit of Holiness by the resurrection from the dead."

In Heb 7. the writer by the Spirit deduces from the silences of the Genesis record in chapter 14 concerning Melchizedek's parentage, etc., a likeness between him and the Son of God. As far as the record goes the King of Salem was "without father, without mother, without descent, (lit. genealogy), having neither beginning of days nor end of life, but made like unto the Son of God." (Heb 7. 3). The great point of similarity, really the *only* point emphasized, is the idea of eternal continuance, both in the past and in the future. Such qualities could not properly be predicated of the Lord in His humanity, as such. The facts are against it. Certainly our Lord had no earthly father, but by Jewish law Joseph became His legal father. Certainly He was not without mother, nor was He "without descent," for the word is as above "without genealogy" (see Matt 1. and Luke 3.); as man too he had beginning of days at Bethlehem, and end of days at Calvary. The points of similarity then between Melchizedek and our Lord, do not attach, in any way, to His incarnation, but to His Sonship in a past eternity, which was therefore prior to the other, and in no way dependent on it.

The quotation in Heb 1. 5, though spoken of Christ after His resurrection goes back to a past eternity, for it was *by inheritance* that He obtained the name of Son, more excellent than any angel's, not by incarnation or resurrection, though He has not yet entered into the glorious inheritance, to which as Son He was appointed Heir. Acts 13. 33 seems clearly to refer to Resurrection. In verse 23 the incarnation is referred to "of this Man's seed hath God *raised* (agein. lit. to lead) unto Israel a Saviour." In verse 30 it is a general word for raised (egeirein) the same word as in verse 22 of David's appointment as king, but in verses 33, 34, we have another word *anistesthai*, which is found 11 times in the Acts, of resurrection. As Alford points out "the meaning: raised from the dead," is absolutely required by the context, both because the word is repeated with "from among the dead" (v 34), and because the apostle's emphasis throughout is on the resurrection (v 30) as the supreme fulfilment of God's promises concerning Jesus. The point of the quotation from Isa 55. is the permanence of His resurrection condition, "now no more to return to corruption." In the words "Thou art my Son, etc.," God recognizes the One who had ever been to Him in relation as Son.

Dr Alford fully discusses the force of these words, and while admitting this declarative sense in the New Testament considers that the primary reference of the words in the Psalm is to the Eternal generation of the Son; "to-day" (seemeron) bearing the well-known definite meaning of the *"ever-present now"* of a past eternity. With this view agree a number of well-known writers, both Latin and Greek, as Origen, Athanasius, Basil, Augustine of Hippo, Chrysostom, Eusebius and Cyril of Alexandria; he also refers to Philo of Alexandria, who also attaches the sense of *"the eternal now"* to the word.

It is evident that in no sense did our Lord become in Resurrection for the first time the Son of God, nor yet by human birth, but He who was the Babe of Bethlehem, and Who in bodily form, bearing the scars of Calvary, entered the "Holy places not made with hands," was the same who, as the Eternal Son of God, had in the beginning created the heavens and the earth, and Who "begotten before all worlds," had been "in the beginning with God." (John 1. 2).

10

SUMMARY AND CONCLUSION

WE may remind ourselves in this our closing chapter, that the difficulties involved in such expressions as "the Eternal generation"; or "the communication of the divine essence" need not perplex us. The greatest difficulty would be, were there no difficulties. If we understand so little the processes of human generation, how may we hope to fathom the Divine? But many of the difficulties, no doubt honestly felt by some, are based on fallacies, such as pressing the analogy of human generation; importing into a past eternity ideas of precedence or subsequence, which belong exclusively to time; confusing the original interrelations of Divine Persons with questions of deity, equality, eternity, etc. The new teachers seem to substitute for the Divine Trinity, a triad of Gods: they are in reality, it is to be feared, tri-theists.

It is not that the Scriptures fail to teach the Eternal Sonship to the simple believer, but the wording must be twisted round to fit in with the new "thoughts of men which are vain." Such expressions as those quoted above do not describe a supposed isolated act in the past, but an eternal and essential relation existing between the Father and Son (see, *e.g.*, John 5. 26); and the "Procession of the Spirit" an eternal relation between Him and the other Divine Persons (John 15. 26). It was not a solitary act which supervened, but a condition which necessarily existed in the Divine Being. The Son is necessarily the Brightness (lit. outshining) of the Divine glroy, as the photosphere may be regarded as a necessary condition of the Sun's existence.

The testimony of the Father from heaven, This is my Beloved Son, at the Jordan, and the Holy Mount is adduced to prove that the Divine Sonship began at Bethlehem, but the logic of this does not lie on the surface. It is quite simple to understand the words as a divine testimony that the humbled One – Jesus, was none other than the Eternal Son. The words no more deny this, than the father's "This my son" of Luke 15. 24 deny that the relation of son already existed.

If the Sonship of our Lord depended on His incarnation, how could Mark, who from the first indicates that his Gospel was "the Gospel of Jesus Christ – the Son of God," make no specific reference to the human birth? nor could John, whose defined object it was to prove the Divine Sonship, *i.e.,* that "Jesus is the Christ – the Son of God" (Chap 20. 31), refrain from referring to it in plain terms.

Moreover, if our Lord's incarnation introduced into the Trinity entirely new relations, it would be, not an emptying, but a filling; not a humbling, but an exaltation; not a revelation of God, but a revolution in God. It is incredible that any such radical changes could take place in the inner relations of the Unchangeable God. The incarnation did reveal what was there before, it could not create entirely new relations. Our Lord's transcendental attributes did not issue from His human birth alone, though by the operation of the Holy Spirit, else His humanity had been unreal, but from the fact that the Person, who entered into Manhood was Divine.

Thus, human birth does not constitute "sons" but "children"; and this is consistently true in the New Testament use of "child" and "son," in the Spiritual sense. The term child denotes relationship; son, known and enjoyed relationship. One is born a child; one becomes a son.

Human birth does not make a child *one with* its father, yet the Lord in John 10. 30 claims this as Son of God (see v 36) – "I and my Father are one," connecting it with Himself as the one "whom the Father hath sanctified and sent into the world."

Nor can the child, by the mere fact of birth, do its father's works, but "the Son" could His Father's (John 5. 19).

Nor does human birth make a child *equal with* its father, yet the Lord claimed this: "My Father worketh hitherto and I work." (John 5. 17). The Jews understood it so, "because He said that God was His (Gk. idios: His own) Father, making Himself equal with God." (John 5. 18). Our Lord did not deny the inference, though he explained that this equality was of a kind not incompatible with subordination (v 19). Nor does human birth confer on a child *equal honours* with its father; yet these the Lord claims for Himself, as Son, a relation which must therefore have existed apart from incarnation. The same may be said of such divine attributes as the omnipotence of v 19, and "the possession of life in Himself" of v 26, which belong to Him, not in virtue of the incarnation, but as the Divine Son.

We may now enquire whether the testimonies to Christ as the Son of God during His ministry were in the Gospels based on the fact of the Virgin Birth? the answer is – Never. The testimonies of fallen spiritual powers to the Sonship were frequent, but we seek in vain for one hint that such knowledge, as they possessed was connected with the Virgin birth. Had they recognized this as the determinant factor, as we are asked to do to-day, they would have referred to it, whereas they seem rather to have been convinced by our Lord's personal qualities and powers. At the temptation Satan sought for proofs of quite a different order, "If thou be the Son of God, command that these stones be made bread," etc., etc. It was the personal glory of Christ which convinced him and the demons that Jesus of Nazareth was indeed that Divine Being, whom they knew and had reason to fear, as the Son of God (see 8. 29; Mark 3. 11; Luke 4. 3, 9, 41; 8. 28; John 6. 69; 11. 27).

Never is the Lord recorded as basing His claims to Divine Sonship on His incarnation nor did He once refer to it. It is, of course, possible that John the Baptist had heard of it from his mother, Elizabeth, though it is an unlikely secret for a mother to confide to her young son. It needed the voice from heaven, and the promised sign of the descent of the Spirit, in form like a dove, to convince him that He who was his younger cousin according to the flesh was indeed the Son of God.

It was clearly no knowledge of the Virgin Birth that led Nathaniel to cry "Thou art the Son of God." (John 1. 49). There is indeed no proof that Philip knew of it himself; certainly there is no mention of his having divulged it to Nathaniel.

It was the display of Christ's omniscience that convicted this latter of His Divine Sonship. The same holds good of the disciples in the storm; they knew nothing of the circumstances of His birth, but they saw His omnipotence writ large in His power over the waves, and accordingly acknowledged Him as Son of God. Had Peter received his knowledge of Christ as Son of God, from Mary, the Lord's mother, it would have been "flesh and blood" that had revealed it to him, but this Christ specifically rules out, and ascribes it to the revelation of His Father in heaven; and so with the Centurion at the cross, and every other witness to His Divine Sonship, recorded in the Scriptures, including that of Thomas after His resurrection. It was by the resurrection that to this last-named apostle, as to numberless others since, Jesus was declared with power to be the Son of God.

Surely were the Human birth the crucial event – the crisis, in the sense which this theory demands, it must have been prominent in every Gospel and Epistle, instead of being mentioned so sparingly. Did the Lord's Divine Sonship result from the miraculous conception, both would be linked in equal prominence and frequency.

That our Lord might share in true and spotless humanity certainly His miraculous birth was indispensible, but these other glories rest on something on an altogether different plane. Did the Lord who claims equal honours with the Father, never enjoy them till He entered into manhood? Such a theory almost makes His Deity depend on His incarnation. Again how impossible to limit such words as "My Father worketh hitherto and I work" to a time subsequent to the incarnation! as though God's rest had not been broken till then. The incarnation could not exhaust the deep meaning of such words as "If God were your Father ye would love Me, for I proceeded forth and came from God; neither came I of myself, but He sent Me" (John 8. 42), or "Say ye of Him Whom the Father hath sanctified and sent into the world, etc." (chap 10 36), or again, "I came forth from the Father, and am come into the world, etc," (chap 16. 28). Or, "Father glorify Thou Me with the glory which I had with Thee before the world was." (chap 17. 5). What deadly darkness must have fallen upon the minds of men, to deny in spite of such Scriptures, the Eternal Fatherhood of God, and the Eternal Sonship of the Lord!

As Bellet has well said "How fearful we should be, lest we admit of any confession of faith (rather indeed of unbelief) that would defraud the Divine bosom of its eternal ineffable delights, and which should tell our God He knew not a Father's joy, and would tell our Lord that He knew not a Son's joy in that bosom from all eternity."

Again he asks, "Can the love of God be understood according to Scripture, if this Sonship be not owned? Does not the love get its character from that very doctrine – "God so loved the world that He gave His only begotten Son"? Does not this love lose its unparalleled glory if this truth be questioned?

To a mind delivered from mere human reasonings (how distinct these are from reasons!) and subject simply to the

Word of God, how clearly such words speak, as "God gave His only begotten Son," "God sent His only begotten Son into the world that we might live through Him!"

APPENDIX ON LUKE 1. 35.

GABRIEL'S words in Luke 1. 35, especially the concluding sentence:– *"Therefore also* that holy thing which shall be born of thee shall be called (the) Son of God," are used to support the new theory, that the Sonship of our Lord Jesus Christ dated from His birth at Bethlehem. What then is the logical force of the "therefore," or the reason that the "also" is introduced? We have already seen that the fact of the bestowal of a name or title in the Word of God in no way precludes the previous existence of the quality or relation so described, as Isa. 9. 6 proves. The names "Wonderful, Counsellor," etc., were not new attributes of the "Son given," but would be vested in Him for the first time as "the child born." The "therefore" goes back naturally to the preceding sentence, in which there are two distinct facts:– the coming on Mary of the Holy Ghost, in view of the conception of the humanity of Christ, and also the separate fact of her being overshadowed[1] by the Power of the Highest. This last is no mere repetition of the former phrase, but an additional statement, that at the moment of the conception, the Divine Logos, the Eternal Son, as we believe, united Himself for ever with the newly created humanity of Christ, and thus entered into manhood. If the Lord were called "Son of God" on account of His Divinely conceived Humanity, then in the same respect in which our Lord was the Son of God, the Spirit would be the Father.

---

[1] Used in Septuagint of the cloud abiding (shah-chan) on the tabernacle (Exod 40. 35).

But He is never thus entitled, therefore Christ is never called the Son of God in His relation as man to the Divine producer of His manhood, to which the agency of the Spirit was confined. To make the expression "Son" attach merely to the humanity of Christ, is to make someone of something and to attach to Him a double Personality. We must therefore refer back His title to be "called Son of God," not to the operation of the Holy Spirit, but to the intervening phrase – "the Power of the Highest shall overshadow thee."

Christ:
The Interpreter
of
The Father

Christ:

The Interpreter

of

The Father

1

IN THE WORLD

"No man hath seen God at any time, the Only begotten Son, who is in the bosom of the Father, He hath declared Him" (John 1.18).

THE word here translated "declared" is often used in Greek writings of the interpretation of things sacred, and divine – oracles, visions, dreams, and is that from which our word "exegesis" is derived.

The exegesis of a passage is its interpretation, as distinct from its application. The Lord Jesus interprets the Father; the Holy Ghost applies the truth to our souls throughout the Word, and we interpret it, for better or worse, in our lives, that "if any obey not the Word, they may be won without the word," like worldly husbands by godly wives (1 Pet 3. 1). A Christ-like life is the soundest of arguments; while an inconsistent life nullifies all arguments.

"No man hath seen God at any time." There were *Theophanies* in the Old Testament, that is, appearances of God, under the temporary disguise of human form, as to

Abraham, Jacob, Joshua, and Daniel. But God as such was never seen. "God is Spirit," (John 4.24m) "dwelling in the light which no man can approach unto, whom no man hath seen, nor can see, to whom be honour and power everlasting" (1 Tim 6. 16). Why cannot I see God? querulously asked the sceptic. "Are you sure you could bear to see Him?" was the reply. "You cannot look at the sun, but God is greater than the sun." Israel "saw the glory of Jehovah"; indeed, it is said, "They saw the God of Israel," but to avoid misconception Moses impressed on them that though the Lord spake unto them out of the midst of the fire, and they heard the voice of the words, they "saw no *similitude*" (Deut 4. 12). Let them take heed not to corrupt themselves by making graven images to represent what they had never seen (4. 15), and so fall where the heathen fell, of whom we read, "When they knew God, they glorified Him not as God . . . but changed the glory of the incorruptible God into an image, made like to corruptible man and to birds and four-footed beasts and creeping things. Wherefore God also gave them up . . . to dishonour their own bodies between themselves" (Rom 1. 23). They degraded God; He let them degrade themselves. If the witness of creation to the eternal power and Godhead of the Creator suffices to condemn the heathen, who make idols of the Deity, what must be the responsibility of those who, in the full blaze of Christianity, represent God in image, picture, and painted window?

Moses himself desired to see God. "I beseech Thee shew me Thy glory," (Ex 33. 18) but instead, God shewed him His "goodness," for He said, "Thou canst not see My face, for there shall no man see Me, and live." (Ex 33. 20). Moses had to rest content to see His "back parts," the "goodness" of God, as revealed in His Name. "The Lord, the Lord God, merciful and gracious, long-suffering and abundant in goodness and truth . . . and that will by no means clear the guilty" (Ex 34. 6, 7). But the key to all this was withheld, and can only be found in a crucified and risen Saviour. There was then a lesser glory which could be seen; a higher, which was unapproachable to the creature. But "God, who commanded the light to shine out of darkness, hath shined in our hearts, to give the light of the knowledge of the glory of God, in the face of Jesus Christ" (2 Cor 4. 6).

There can be little question that the appearance of Jehovah in Old Testament times in human form, or under the semblance of fire as in the bush, or in the Shekinah, were through the same glorious Person. Jehovah of the Old Testament is Jesus of the New. He was "the brightness of His glory," before He became "the express image (Greek, *character*, impress) of His Person" (Heb 1. 3); the *appearance* of the Invisible God before He became His image (Greek, *eikon*).

The first mention of the glory of Jehovah is in Exod 16. Two gifts were bestowed on Israel, "at even" and "in the morning," and with a different purpose. "At even, then *ye shall know* that the Lord hath brought you out of the land of Egypt" (v 6). This came true in the gift of the quails — natural food, material mercies, providentially supplied, easily understood, and very cheering in the wilderness journey. Provision by the way is intended to assure our hearts, that the Lord has put us in the way. But there was something else. "In the morning then *ye shall see* the glory of the Lord" (v 7). This was fulfilled next day, when "upon the face of the wilderness there lay a small round thing as the hoar frost." They called it "manna," "for they wist not what it was," (Ex 16. 14, 15) and, alas! soon tired of it. This was a higher thing than the quails, it was a heavenly nourishment: "He gave them bread from heaven to eat"; "Man did eat angels' food." As the old corn of the land they fed on later, is a symbol of Christ in resurrection glory, so is this of Jesus in humiliation, "the Bread of God which cometh down from heaven and giveth life unto the world" (John 6. 33). But He was unrecognised, misunderstood, and hated. "The world knew Him not." "His own received Him not. But as many as received Him, to them gave He power to become the children of God, even to them that believe on His Name" (John 1. 12). All such, the apostle linked with himself, when he testified, "The Word was made flesh and tabernacled among us, and *we* beheld His glory, the glory of the only begotten of the Father, full of grace and truth" (v 14m). This glory was not, as I judge, the glory manifested on the transfiguration mount, but the *moral* glory of His Person.

One grand purpose of the incarnation was to reveal the Father, and who could do this but He who had eternal knowledge of Him, being Himself the eternal Son – the Word who was "in the beginning" – and eternally in relation to Him? Who but a Divine Being could accurately know a Divine Person? for no man knoweth "the Father save the Son, and he to whomsoever the Son will reveal Him." (Matt 11. 27). Who is qualified to interpret the Father, save He who is "in the bosom of the Father"? No created being – cherubim, seraphim, archangel, or angel – could take that place, save He who is "the only begotten Son." He only could learn the secrets of the Father's heart, and interpret them to us. Would we learn "the secret of the Lord," then we too must lean upon His breast, like the beloved disciple. Would we know the Father? then we must trace the pathway of Him who, while He walked the earth, was yet in heaven (chap 3. 14), considering His ways, His works, and words, for all were the reflection of the Father's will. "The Son can do nothing of Himself, but what He seeth the Father do" (John 5. 19). "As I hear I judge" (John 5. 30). "My doctrine is not Mine, but His that sent Me" (John 7. 16). "He that hath seen ME hath seen the Father" (John 14. 7). Not that they were the same, but that His every act, was the fulfilment of the Father's purpose, every word the echo of His command, every step the effect of His leading, and all His ways the unfolding of God's great heart of love.

2

IN A SCENE OF SIN (John 1)

THE ministry of John, naturally aroused deep searchings of heart. Who could he be who drew such vast crowds into the wilderness, and of whom all bare witness that he was a prophet? When the Jews sent priests and Levites to ask him who he was, "he confessed and denied not (that is, he did not refuse to answer), but confessed, I am not the Christ" (John 1. 19, 20). Their further question was a tacit acknowledgment of his greatness. If he were not the Christ, he might be either Elias or the prophet to arise like Moses; he could be no one less. The answer of John was surprising. He made no claim to be anything but "a voice," the herald of Another, "who coming after him was preferred before him," the latchet of whose shoes he was unworthy to unloose. Who could this august personage be? None other than Jehovah – the God of Israel, for the message of the voice was, "Make straight the way of THE LORD" (see Isa 40. 3).

Even John had failed to recognise in his cousin, "Jesus," anything more than the holiest of men, of whom he needed to be baptised, rather than Jesus to be baptised of him. But since that memorable moment, when the promised sign was fulfilled, and the Holy Spirit descended like a dove and rested upon Him, he knew Him as the Baptiser in the Holy Spirit – the Son of God. It is important to note the character in which the Lord first presented Himself to Israel, for this must throw a vivid light on the purpose of His mission, and correspond too with the deepest need of men. Some would represent the world specially as a "troubled sea, when it cannot rest," (Isa 57. 20) or as a scene of sorrow, suffering, and death; but Christ saw it under a more serious aspect, which lay at the root of every other woe. It was a place of sin. He came to interpret the heart of God to a world of *sinners.* As He emerged from the hidden ministry of Nazareth into public life, it was in His sacrificial character. "Behold the Lamb of God that taketh away the sin[1] of the world." (John 1. 29). The presence of Jesus as the Lamb of God's providing, revealed the Divine compassion to a sin-stricken world. "The Father sent the Son to be the Saviour of the world" (1 John 4. 14).

A certain ill-omened school of interpretation represents the Cross as an after-thought, a profound disillusionment of our Lord's early hopes, a dire necessity, arising from the failure of His mission. Nothing could be further from the truth. How that death came to pass, did depend on circumstances, but that it should come to pass was inscribed at the head of the Divine programme, unfolding an eternal purpose. This was the primary conception of the mission of Christ. He was the Lamb "fore-ordained, before the foundation of the world, but manifest in these last times" (1 Pet 1. 20), "the Lamb slain from the foundation of the world" (Rev 13. 8). The love of God was thus interpreted as not only toward the faithful patriarchs, "the sons of God" of antedeluvian days, nor merely toward the elect of Israel and of the nations, but to the whole race. He presented Himself as "THE LAMB." This was no unfamiliar thought to Israelites. Here was the antitype of centuries of sin-offerings, "on Jewish altars slain" – "the Lamb of God," not only for an individual, a family, a people, but for the whole world. It has been seriously objected to this interpretation, that it would be an anachronism to credit John with such a clear conception of the Cross. How could he know what was still in the future? It was not unusual in prophets to have a

---

[1] There is a distinction between "sin" and "sins" in the same context, as in John 8. 21, 24, RV, and 1 John 1. 6-9, but I think here, "sin" includes "sins."

knowledge of the future, and John was a prophet, and "more than a prophet." (Matt 11. 9). But in what sense does the Lamb of God take away the sin of the world? Some refer the phrase to "original sin." Christ in His death so fully met the sin of Adam, that its effects are neutralised for all. Were that so, no infant would die. Others connect it with the millennial earth. But though Satan will be banished, sin will not be taken away, as the final rebellion of Revelation (chap 20) proves. The true meaning is, that the sin of the world is taken away, not absolutely, but potentially. If that sin is to be taken away, it is He, and He alone, who must do it.

The Taker Away of Sin. John the Baptist had appeared as the forerunner, "to make ready a people prepared for the Lord." He baptised with the baptism of repentance. Those baptised confessed their guilt, and justified God in His sentence on their sin; but how could that sin be taken away? That, no ordinance could achieve. They must wait for Him that was to come. And when He came, it was not as a Preacher, but as a Saviour; not as an Example, but a Sacrifice; not as the Man of God, but as the Lamb of God – the taker away of the world's sin. The question may arise as to how sin was dealt with in the ages before Christ died. Was it on the ground of works, or of law keeping? This is very important, for if God could pass over sin on such grounds then, why should the death of Christ be necessary for forgiveness now? The answer is, there has never been but one ground on which sin could be passed over, namely, the atonement of Christ.

In old time, God dealt with man in various ways during successive periods known as "dispensations." Man was subjected to different tests, the light of conscience, government, law, the actual presence of Christ in Israel, and all this to bring out what was in him, stop his mouth, and shut him up to grace. But from the fall, approach to God by sacrifice was instituted and continued, like a silver thread, throughout the old economy. Every sacrifice was a fingerpost to Calvary. The elect of all ages bowed to God, and condemned themselves. Even in the absence of literal sacrifices, the principle held good, "the sacrifices of God are a broken spirit: a broken and a contrite heart, O God, Thou wilt not despise" (Psa 51. 17). To such an one, God could apply the value of the future work of Him, who was ever present to His mind as "the Lamb slain." There are two ways in which a man might let a friend buy goods at his expense at one of the great business palaces of London: He might allow him to run up a bill to his account, himself guaranteeing the store payment by a certain date, or he might open a deposit account and allow the friend to draw on it. The saved of Old Testament time were accepted "on credit," if we may so say; those of to-day are in virtue of the price already paid at Calvary. The *ground* in any case, on which a sinner is forgiven, is not his acceptance of the work of Christ (that is the necessary act which unites Him to the Saviour), but God's acceptance of that work. All God's holy claims are satisfied, and He has proved it by raising Christ from the dead and giving Him glory.

There are, however, important differences in detail between the past and present dispensations. Then the true ground of justification was not revealed; now the righteousness of God is declared in the Cross. How could God be just in passing over sin, when the blood of bulls and of goats was powerless to take it away? The word used in Rom 3. 25 for "remission," with reference to "the sins that were past," (instead of *aphesis* the usual word) is "letting pass" (*paresis*), a word never used of God's dealing with sins now. The Old Testament saint knew the blessedness of forgiveness (Psa 32. 1), but not the righteous ground. The real transaction at the Cross, revealed a righteous, because sufficient ground, for the putting away of sin. Before, grace had flowed in a narrow channel, now like Jordan, it overflows its banks all the time of the harvest of this Gospel dispensation. Christ is "the Lamb of God that taketh away the sin of the *world*." (John 1. 29).

We may compare this, with other similar phrases in John's Gospel, "That was the true Light, which lighteth every man, that cometh into the world" (chap 1. 9). "The Bread of God, is He which cometh down from heaven and giveth life unto the world" (chap 6. 33). "I, if I be lifted up from the earth, will draw all men unto Me" (chap. 12. 32). All such passages must be interpreted in the potential sense. Not all have been actually enlightened, quickened, or drawn; but Christ is the only Light, the universal Bread, the unique Magnet, the world's Taker Away of sin. None can do it, but He alone. "He is the propitiation for our sins (actual effect); and not for ours only, but also for the whole world" (potential efficacy), (1 John 2. 2 RV). He is sufficient for all, efficient for those who believe. One might point to the parish doctor, or the village blacksmith. This one heals us, that one shoes our horses; but the condition is understood, need experienced, and acceptance of skill in both cases. Where is the eye to turn to the Light, the faith to eat Bread, the will to be drawn, the hand to be laid on the head of the Lamb? This is what John himself did, and the five disciples who came to Jesus – Andrew, Peter, Philip, Nathaniel, and the anonymous one, whom most believe to be the writer, John, himself. Millions have done so since, "and there's room for many more." None have ever ventured on the Lamb of God, but their sins have at once been taken away, and blotted out of the book of God's remembrance.

3

IN A SCENE OF HUMAN JOY (John 2)

THERE are striking parallels between the first chapter of Ezekiel's prophecy and the first chapter of John's Gospel. In both, a prophet-priest, outside the land, receives visions of God from an opened heaven, revealing the glory of the Lord, and both end with a Man upon the throne. This naturally leads on to a marriage feast. At Bethabara the Lord Jesus is seen as "the Lamb of God," interpreting the thoughts of the Father to repentant ones, who had confessed their sins in baptism. At Cana, He appears in quite another character, interpreting the Father to His disciples as the Bountiful Creator, who knows "what things ye have need of, before ye ask Him," (Matt 6. 8) and "giveth us richly all things to enjoy," (1 Tim 6. 17) "filling our hearts with food and gladness." (Acts 14. 17). It is really Psalm 103 followed by Psalm 104. Many would judge the former to be at a higher level than the latter, but the praise of the latter really reaches the higher note. It is not only for what God has done, but for what He is. "Thou art very great." "He" of Psalm 103 becomes "Thou" of Psalm 104. "The Lord" becomes "O Lord, *my* God." There is the joy of forgiveness in Psalm 103. But in Psalm 104 there is the joy of communion, the "wine that maketh glad the heart of man" (v 15). It is this which we have at Cana. It is noteworthy, that the first scene into which the Lord introduced His small nucleus of disciples was a scene of human joy, a marriage feast, thus setting His seal to the institution of Eden, and stamping with His approval the innocent joys even of a fallen earth. It seems a mistake to assert, as some do, that "the first man is gone," for marriage, like eating and drinking, moderate labour, and sleep, belongs to the estate of the first man who is "of the earth, earthy," (1 Cor 15. 47) or, in other words, is "made of earth to dwell on the earth." It is the "old man," not the first man, which is gone for the believer, for that was crucified with Christ. Earthly relationships are not annulled for those who are in Christ, they take on a new and deeper character. Marriage is honourable for all, and "the unbelieving husband is sanctified by the wife;" that is, set apart to her by the divine ordinance of matrimony, and the children are set apart,[1] though in no higher sense, as the fruit of it (1 Cor 7. 14). It is a pathetic fact that however much and often marriage has by human sin proved a failure, a wedding is more than anything else in this sad world an occasion of joy and gladness. If people are not cheerful on their wedding day, when are they likely to be? By the blessing of God, marriage "in the Lord" proves to many a source of happiness and blessing. God thus sets "the solitary in families," (Ps 68. 6) and provides mutual comfort and support for His creatures.

We may take the marriage of Cana as symbolical of kingdom joys in a future day, when again "shall be heard in this place (the land of Israel) . . . the voice of joy, and the voice of gladness, the voice of the bridegroom, and the voice of the bride, the voice of them that shall say, 'Praise the Lord of Hosts: for the Lord is good; for His mercy endureth for ever'" (Jer 33. 10,11). The disciples had "much tribulation" to pass through, before they could enter the Kingdom of God, but on that day at Cana, this was bridged over, and they had a foretaste at the start of their long journey, of the great marriage feast yet to come. Thus He "manifested forth His glory; and His disciples believed on Him" (John 2. 11) – their budding faith broke into blossom. Here then we see our Lord Jesus interpreting the

---

[1] "Holy," as applied to children, is from the same root as "sanctified" of the unbelieving parent, and entails no change of character.

Father's heart in a scene of human gladness, as the friendly Man among men, the kindly neighbour, rejoicing with them that rejoice – not an ascetic like John the Baptist, the Levitical Nazarite, to whom all wine was denied and a life enjoined contrary to nature – mourning to men who would not weep – the frivolous world around; but a true Nazarite of the dispensation of grace, type nearest to the heart of God, partaking of the blessings of this life, when they might offer themselves, piping to men who would not dance – the religious world, who mistake asceticism for devotion to God, because their system is founded on human ordinances. This would be proper to a worldly cult, "touch not; taste not; handle not; which all are to perish with the using; after the commandments and doctrines of men? which things have indeed a shew of wisdom in will worship, and humility, and neglecting of the body but (where we follow the RV) are not of any value against the indulgence of the flesh" (Col 2. 23).

To judge from the map, Cana occupied the very site of Gath-Hepher the city of Jonah the prophet – a fact so strangely ignored by the Pharisees, when they asserted "out of Galilee ariseth no prophet." (John 7. 52). But a greater than Jonah was present that day. He came with His disciples as the invited Guest. It was His wont to accept invitations; indeed, we never hear of His refusing one, whether to the houses of His own people, as Matthew, or Martha, or Simon the leper, or to those of the religious world, like Simon the Pharisee. But wherever He went it was as the Faithful Witness. It may be questioned whether Christians do not sometimes fail through indolence or fear of man, to avail themselves of invitations to the tables of the unconverted, even where they can go without the sacrifice of principle, or to participate in the foolish or sinful pleasures of the world. The question in such cases is not so much where, but how we go. Do I sit merely in fellowship with men, as one of themselves, or as a servant of Christ and a witness for God? "If any of them that believe not, bid you to a feast" (some would say at once, under plea of separation, don't go), but the apostle adds, "and ye be disposed to go (leaving the decision to the conscience of each), whatsoever is set before you, eat, asking no question for conscience sake," (1 Cor 10. 27) but, as the context shows, when principle is involved, standing firm for God.

Thus the Lord interpreted the Father by His condescending and loving interest in the joys of the home and of human friendship, not as on a pedestal of Pharisaic superiority, "Stand by thyself, for I am holier than thou," but as the meek and lowly One, never more morally separated from publicans and sinners, than when receiving them and eating with them.

But the Lord was more than the invited Guest. He became the bountiful Host, dispensing abundant provision to the needy, and that not at the suggestion of Mary – for human relationships, as was proved again in John 7. 6, never might interfere with His service for the Father – but in the Father's own time. Mary, though wrong as to time, was right as to fact. Like the little maid in Naaman's house, who, though she had never heard of a leper being cleansed, knew that the prophet of God could and would heal her master, so Mary, though she had never seen one miracle wrought in all the long years at Nazareth, knew He was the one to appeal to, and could and would supply the need. She was not discouraged by the seeming failure of her request; she knew His hour would come, and so gave her memorable advice to the servants – so timely for all of us – "Whatsoever He saith unto you, do it." (John 2. 5). And when His hour did come, He knew what to do and how to do it. He stored His wine, not in wine jars, but in strange receptacles, in water-pots, each holding about twenty-one gallons, set for ceremonial cleansing, so needful in a scene of defilement, under an earthly system of religion. But the water-pots were empty, fit symbol of the emptiness of the forms they represented. But our Lord had them filled to the brim with water, to turn it into His wine. Thus He displayed the omnipotence of the Creator. The God of nature, the Lord of the vintage, laid aside the leisurely processes, so familiar to us, and peformed in a moment what He usually did in months. Exactly when the water became wine, we are not told; it became so for practical use, when the servants obeyed the command, "Draw out now"! (John 2. 8). The wine is there if we will but draw it out and serve to the thirsty around. The secret of the Lord was with the servants. They knew, for they feared and obeyed. The governor of the feast tasted and wondered, but did he ever learn whence the good wine flowed? In any case, the Lord interpreted the loving-kindness of the Father for those who had eyes to see. To such He would say, "Your Father knoweth that ye have need of these things." (Luke 12. 30). The act was symbolical. How many are taught to say, "Thy love is better than wine" (SoS 1. 2) – "we will remember thy love more than wine: the upright love thee," (SoS 1. 4). How often the waters of affliction are turned into the wine of joy! As Samuel Rutherford wrote, "When I get into the cellar of affliction, I search round for some of the Lord's wine." Joy is the second of the ninefold fruit of the Spirit from Him who is the Fountain of it, but lack of love here, often turns the good wine sour, and so spoils that which makes glad the heart of God and man. But surely the testimony of the redeemed of the Lord in heaven will be, "Thou hast kept the good wine until now." (John 2. 10).

4

IN A SCENE OF SUFFERING (John 5)

THE soil of a sin-blighted world, is more congenial to suffering than to joy. Cana feasts are rare oases. Joy is an exotic. Sickness and pain are indigenous. "The whole creation groaneth and travaileth in pain together until now." (Rom 8. 22). The great multitude at the pool of Bethesda, "impotent" and "waiting," is a fair sample of this world. (John 5.1-9). What, then, was our Lord's attitude to suffering, during His earthly ministry? How did He interpret the Father? That He should come where sufferers were, says much, but once there, He could not be indifferent. Compassion was a keynote of His ministry. But what drew it out of Him, would repel others; a man full of leprosy (Mark 1. 41); a man full of demons (Mark 5. 19); a Jew full of enmity (Luke 10. 33); a selfish crowd, whom He had served all day, breaking in on His rest. Here, toward the sufferers, lying in their filth and misery at Bethesda, He was no doubt moved with the same compassion, thus interpreting the heart of Him who is "full of compassion" – "The Father of mercies and the God of all comfort" (2 Cor 1. 3). For us, too, "His compassions fail not," (Lam 3.22) "for we have not an High Priest which cannot be touched with the feeling of our infirmities" (Heb 4. 15). A feast was the occasion of the Bethesda miracle, one of the three great annual feasts, we may suppose, to necessitate our Lord's presence in Jerusalem, but which, is unimportant. Whatever it might be to the mass of the Jews, to Him it would be "a feast of Jehovah," and no doubt all the legal requirements of the day in their very spirit were observed by Him. In what house of feasting would He then be found? Rather in a house of mourning, the porches of Bethesda, where "lay a great multitude of impotent folk, of blind, halt, withered waiting for the moving of the water." (v 3). Little enough of feasting had come their way, but now the Lord of the feast was present. His disciples had accompanied Him to the marriage feast; here He would seem to be alone, perhaps He could not trust them in such a scene. This "great multitude" may represent the religious world, especially Israel under law, helpless and hopeless, and dependent for blessing on irregular interventions of Divine favour, the visits of the angel of the Lord.[1] But a greater was present that day, unrecognised, but ready to bless, the Lord of the "angel." Had some sufferer been praying with the psalmist, "Shew us Thy mercy, O Lord, and grant us Thy salvation"! (Psa 85. 7) the answer would have been doubly appropriate, "Surely His salvation is nigh them that fear Him." (Psa 85.9). Jesus was in their midst. They need not wait. He could do for them, then and there, as for us, above their highest prayer and thought. And why was He there? Not to apologise for God for all the suffering in the world, nor to deny its reality with that spurious "science" falsely-called "Christian," nor yet to preach the counterfeit gospel of future bliss by present pain, nor even to introduce improved hygienic conditions or schemes of social betterment (doubtless much needed) for the sufferers around the pool. Physical needs are not ignored by Christianity, but higher needs must be kept first. The world has copied the social activities of Christians: hospitals,

---

[1] The latter part of verse 3 and the whole of verse 4 are omitted by the Sinaitic and Vatican and Cambridge Uncial MSS, and some other weighty authorities, but are retained in the Alexandrine (London) and other Uncials, and some versions of good authority. The reply of the impotent in verse 7, is undisputed. What sense would this have, were the disputed words in 3 and 4 not genuine? He was in a great hurry to get into the pool when troubled, but who could tell what was meant, if the previous reference was absent.

orphanages, etc., while denying their motive power – the faith of Christ. Why then was the Lord there? First and foremost to do the will of the Father, in this work of mercy, symbolical of the excellence of grace over law. "What the law could not do, in that it was weak through the flesh, God sending His own Son," (Rom 8. 3) could do. The law could point the moral of their sad estate, but was powerless to "raise the fallen, cheer the faint, heal the sick, or lead the blind." Christ alone could do all this, and He is there to do it, wherever there is human need. He is still at faith's disposal, near and ready to save and bless.

Christ as the Healer. This opens out an important enquiry as to the "limitations" imposed on our Lord's ministry of healing. Certainly there was no limitation as to power. Had not He who had "life in Himself," power over all disease and death? Must not all suffering therefore flee before Him? We do not find it so. His compassion and power did not express themselves in indiscriminate relief. The Son of God was manifested to destroy "the works of the devil" (1 John 3. 8), but these must not be confused with the *effects* of sin. Sin and sins are the works of the devil; sickness and suffering are effects of sin, for the race directly, for the individual sometimes directly, but more often indirectly, as in the case of the blind man of the 9th of John, for the glory of God, "that the works of God might be made manifest in him." (v 3). This should comfort those exposed to the erroneous teaching, that all sickness is a proof of unbelief, if not of positive sin in the sufferer. In such circles, bodily healing is the pivot of true religion, the hall mark of genuine faith. But this shows an ill-balanced grasp of the truth, a feeble sense of spiritual values. Physical healing was an accessory, not the essence of our Lord's ministry; a credential of His Messiahship, not like the resurrection, the crowning witness to His eternal Sonship. His miracles were a divine seal to His claims, and also to the testimony of His apostles, "God also bearing them witness, both with signs and wonders and with divers miracles and gifts of the Holy Ghost according to His own will" (Heb 2. 4). Had He willed it, such signs would have continued. We have as a permanent witness, the record of them, as also of the star of Bethlehem, the herald angels, the resurrection, and the tongues at Pentecost. Far be it for us to discourage "faith in God;" we need more of it, in sickness as in health. But faith, based on a defective interpretation of the Word of God, easily becomes presumption and fanaticism. "Faith healers" seek to attach a Satanic stigma to all medicines by dubbing them "drugs" and "not of God." Did Satan give to these their healing properties, or are they, no less than the foods we eat, "creations of God," to be received "with thanksgiving?" (1 Tim 4.4). There is no antithesis between Divine healing and the use of "means." Even in James 5. 14, the word "anoint" is the mundane word *aleiphein* – not the sacred word *chriein* (lit. 'touch with hand') of religious anointings. Oil was and is recognised as a healing agent, in many countries. Was there ever a more direct Divine healing than that of Hezekiah? Fanaticism would have refused the fig plaster prescribed by Isaiah, but faith accepted and applied it. Now, some tell us, that if we use "means," we run the risk of denying the Name of the Lord as Jehovah-Ropheka – I am the Lord that healeth thee. But it has to be remembered that this promise was conditional – not on prayer and faith – but on obedience to Jehovah's commandments. And the promise was not the cure of sickness when ill, but an immunity from it altogether. It is surely noteworthy that so radically an anti-Christian sect as "Christian Science," already referred to, undoubtedly is, while denying the Person and Work of Christ in any Scriptural sense, should appeal to New Testament miracles to substantiate their own claims to heal; "Christ and His apostles did it, why not we?" they argue, "we are therefore a divine revelation." But miracles may be Satanic, for the Antichrist will work miracles by the power of the dragon

113

(Rev 13. 12-15). To remove by an act of power all the effects of sin, would neither be righteous or beneficial, and God nowhere pledges Himself to do it. That depends as far as man is concerned, on his attitude to God and his faith in Christ. In the dire effects of sin, we read its exceeding gravity. Suffering may lead sinners to God (Job 33. 19-24), and if rightly borne, conforms the Christian to the image of Christ, and yields "the peaceable fruit of righteousness." (Heb 12.11). The devil and his works have been judicially destroyed[2] by the death of Christ. It is only a question of time for this to be manifest to all. This disposes of the mistaken notion that sinning will continue for ever in the regions of the lost. The sinful nature will be unchanged, the will to sin as determined as ever, but never will one more commission of sin be permitted in the Universe, when once the lake of fire has closed on the impenitent. It would be a defective system, which allowed criminals to commit in prison, the acts which brought them there.

Besides the general considerations already referred to, as affecting the question of healing, which hold good for all time, there were definite bounds, mostly temporary in character, within which the exercise of our Lord's miraculous powers, was limited. But here we must define our terms. How could a Divine Person be limited? The limitations were not of His powers, but of their exercise, not imposed, but voluntarily accepted, not of ignorance or inability, but of reserve and self-restraint. The Lord Jesus did not cease to be God, or to exist as God, when He took "the form of a servant," (Phil 2. 7) and became man. He retained everything essential to true Deity, while refusing nothing proper to perfect humanity. But in not insisting on the retention of what He had always possessed by His very nature, equality with God, "He emptied Himself," (Phil 2. 7

---

[2] Not annihilated, but annulled, or rendered ineffective (cf Rom 3. 3; 4. 14; 1 Cor. 1. 28, etc.).

114

RV) and that not by relinquishing His Divine attributes, which would have entailed emptying Himself of Himself – an impossibility – but as the following phrase of Philippians 2 explains, by "taking upon Him the form of a servant." He did not cease to be what He had always been, but entered into a new relation to the Father, which meant, holding both Divine and human attributes, to use them not from Himself, but as the bondslave of the Father; consenting to live henceforth as the dependent One, never to move, speak, or act, except at His bidding. We know where that obedience led Him, even to "the death of the Cross." (v 8) There, He fully glorified the Father, met every claim against the sinner, and bore His peoples' sins. Is the Lord Jesus to be the only one to follow this path of dependence? No, all true service is on the same principle.

Satan, who had the highest place as servant in heaven, revolted against the will of God, and entered the path of self-will, which could only lead to eternal judgment and abasement. The Lord took the lowest place as Servant on earth, became subject to the will of God in all things, fully glorified Him before the universe, and will ever occupy the highest place in the glory, as the Son of Man. He thus became the faithful Interpreter of the Father's will, accepting all the circumstances of His choice. By the first of these, He was conditioned as man.

1. Geographically and Ethnically. – He was brought up in a despised city of Galilee, instead of at Jerusalem, "the Holy City," the centre of Rabbinnical learning. His sphere of service, instead of being worldwide, was confined to a small country, much the size of Wales. His mission, instead of being to every creature, was to "the lost sheep of the house of Israel." Instead of claiming the universal throne, He was satisfied to present Himself as the heir to David's throne.

2. Practically. – Even in His testimony to Israel His service was confined within the circle of the Divine plan. He made no claim to initiative. He did the works prepared for Him, and no other. "The Son can do nothing of Himself, but what He seeth the Father do." (John 5. 19). "As I hear I judge." (John 5. 30). "My doctrine is not mine, but His that sent Me." (John 7. 16). His whole life was the interpretation of the Father's purpose. Outside this limit, no miracles were performed. But this purpose was no arbitrary one. It was already revealed in principle in the prophetic Word.

3. Prophetically. – "He was a minister of the circumcision for the truth of God, to confirm the promises made unto the fathers" (Rom 15. 8). We read for example, "He healed all that were sick, that it might be fulfilled, which was spoken by Esaias the prophet, saying, Himself took our infirmities and bare our sicknesses" (Matt 8. 17). Earlier, we learn that His movements were regulated by that same Word "He came and dwelt in Capernaum . . . that it might be fulfilled, which was spoken by Esaias the prophet" (Matt 4. 14; Isa 9. 1, 2). A Messiah without miracles could not be the Messiah of prophecy. They were His necessary credentials, and thus, in the synagogue of Nazareth, he applied Isa 61. 1 to Himself with the words, "This day is this Scripture fulfilled in your ears." "Not eyes," for they had seen no miracles, but the fame of Capernaum had reached their ears. Later, it was by appeal to His miracles (not to the signs at His baptism) that He confirmed the faith of John in prison.

4. Ethically. – The moral condition of men influenced his miraculous ministry (Matt 13. 58). Faith favoured, unbelief obstructed it. "He could not do many mighty works there, because of their unbelief." "If thou canst believe, all things are possible to him that believeth" (Mark 9. 23). His works demanded a certain moral attitude in those needing healing. Thus, He put out the scorners (Mark 5. 40); He led the blind man out of Bethsaida, the scene in vain of so many wonderful works (Mark 8. 23). And His miracles in Jerusalem, the city of rejection, were but few. The one man healed at Bethesda fulfilled at any rate two conditions – he was helpless and he knew it; he did what he was told, and so shewed his faith.

5. Dispensationally. – Some who are more exhorters than teachers – are impatient of dispensational teaching, lest Christians be robbed of the practical application of Scripture, as for instance of the "Sermon on the Mount."[3] But in reality, it is only as taken in its dispensational setting, that a true application can be made of any Scripture. "Distinguish the dispensations, and the Scriptures agree," as Augustine has it. Interpret according to dispensation, then apply to present circumstances according to the analogy of the faith. Had these simple principles been grasped, how much misapplication of Scripture would have been prevented. Thus, why are there only three miracles of healing described by John, whereas the Synoptists abound in such? The answer lies in the dispensational character of the latter. For instance, in the period from Matt 4. 23 to 9. 35, embracing our Lord's great personal kingdom testimony, the historical record presents us with one succession of miracles, calculated to convince the nation that "the Kingdom of God was come unto them" (Matt 12. 28). This period ends with the rejection of the testimony by the leaders of the nation, ascribing to Satan the miracles of Christ (chap 9. 34). In chap 10. the Lord associates the twelve with Himself, the testimony widens, but ends in the same rejection. The people come to the right conclusion, "Is not this the Son of David," that is, "Is not this the rightful heir to David's throne?" but the conviction is at once quenched by the same blasphemous suggestion (chap 12.

---

[3] Eg – As regards Matt 5. 5, the Christian is not encouraged to be meek by the promise of inheriting the earth. That is the hope of Israel. The inheritance of the believer is now "reserved in heaven," which cannot mean an earthly inheritance reserved in heaven, but a heavenly inheritance. The Christian is to be meek, so as to walk worthy of his high calling (Eph 4. 2).

24). Thus the kingdom is rejected, and the testimony takes on a new character. Parables, we may almost say, henceforth replace miracles. Why – if as some assert – there be no break at chap 12, the change in the testimony, and why do miracles henceforth take a secondary place?

What a contrast, indeed, between Matthew and John! In the former Gospel, our Lord is more than accessible. He seeks out the sufferer. No ones and twos are healed, but multitudes. "All manner of sickness and all manner of disease," (Matt 4. 23) "all sick people," (Matt 4. 24) "healing every sickness and every disease," (Matt 9. 35) are phrases characteristic of its early chapters. In John, the miracles are few and far between. The key is close at hand. The testimony in Matthew is a kingdom and therefore a miraculous testimony. In John, there is no proclamation of the kingdom. John begins where the Synoptists only arrive, when well on their way, with rejection. We read Calvary in the words, "His own received Him not" (John 1. 12). This gospel presents Him as the Lamb of God which taketh away the sin of the world.

The same phenomenon is seen in the course of the Acts. Miraculous intervention are plentiful at the beginning – because there the presentations of the kingdom in the Jewish sense are specially to the fore, but as the testimony changes, so does the miraculous fade away. This would account for the fact that in "The prison epistles," (Ephesians, Philippians, Colossians, and Philemon) in which the "mystery" is officially revealed, there is not a word about miracles. And those who expect them now "do err, not knowing the Scriptures," (Matt 22. 29) or their place in the dispensations of God.

Until the last enemy has been destroyed and the kingdom be restored in enhanced splendour to God, even the Father (1 Cor 15. 24), there will still be sickness and suffering in the world. Those called to pass through these trying experiences, may surely cry for relief to the Good Physician, and also seek the fellowship of their brethren in prayer, while not neglecting the common sense precautions and remedies, which it has pleased God to place within their reach. But if He be not pleased to bless the means used, or deliver from the infirmity, His presence and sympathy are assured. And His promise remains, "My grace is sufficient for thee: for My strength is made perfect in weakness." (2 Cor 12. 9).

5

IN A SCENE OF NEED (John 6)

THE miracle of the feeding of the five thousand is unique, in being the only one – if we except of course the crowning miracle of the resurrection – which is narrated in all the four Gospels. There must be teaching of special importance to be learnt from it. The sister miracle of "the four thousand" is given in Matthew 15 and Mark 8. Probably had our Lord Himself not settled the matter otherwise (Matt 16. 9, 10), the critics would have asserted in their lofty fashion, the identity of the two miracles. Perhaps they have done so, for modern Sadducees that they are, their *forte* is knowledge of their own writings rather than of the Holy Scriptures.

The fact that two distinct miracles were performed, so closely similar, may throw light on some of what are termed "the discrepancies of the Gospels." Perhaps we have too readily assumed the identity of incidents, which, though similar, are after all distinct. In the miracle before us, the Lord is presented as interpreting the Father in a scene of human need, as the One who opens His hand and satisfieth "the desire of every living thing," (Psa 145. 16) and who knows and forestalls His people's wants, before they ask Him. In each of the synoptists the occasion is the same. The evil curiosity of Herod had been aroused, by the fame of Jesus. "It is John, whom I beheaded;" (Mark 6. 16), and, he "desired to see Him." (Luke 9. 9). But the Lord withdraws Himself from the inquisitiveness of the proud, and reveals Himself to the humble seeker. "He hath filled the hungry with good things; but the rich He hath sent empty away." (Luke 1. 53). The twelve had just returned from their mission. He knew their frame, they were weary and needed rest. "Come ye yourselves apart," He said, "into a desert place and rest awhile; for there were many coming and going, and they had no leisure so much as to eat". (Mark 6. 31). Accordingly they took shipping to a desert spot on the northern shore of the lake; but the people passed round the lake on foot, and outwent them. The place belonged to Bethsaida (Luke 9. 10), the scene of so many miracles (Matt 11. 21). The city was to witness perhaps, one more appeal to their repentance and faith. Instead then of a place of peace and repose, it was a scene of hustle and confusion which our Lord and His disciples found on landing. The very crowds they had been ministering to, and had been obliged to leave for quietness sake, were there awaiting them. What would be our Lord's attitude to these men? Fallen human nature would have become testy and irritable. Did He reproach them for their selfishness and lack of consideration to Him and His tired disciples? Nay, for in Him we see perfection. "He was moved with compassion toward them, because they were as sheep not having a shepherded" (not first because they were physically needy, but without spiritual guidance), "and He began to teach them many things" (Mark 6. 34) and then, as Matthew tells us, He "healed their sick" (chap 16. 14).

Next arose the problem of food. Our Lord's question to Philip seems to have been a private one. The Lord had Himself called Philip, perhaps there was a special link between his Lord and him, a peculiar desire on the part of Christ to see him grow in grace.

A natural thought, when we see a crowd, is how will their needs be catered for. When the Lord saw one, He made their needs His own. How shall *we* cater for them? "Whence shall *we* buy bread that these may eat?" (John 6. 5). Philip's difficulty was not so much whence, but how. He names an unheard of sum, far beyond the resources of their common bag. But even that would not be sufficient. Our Lord's question to Philip was "to prove him: for He Himself knew what He would do." (v 6). The Lord has ways outside our ken. His resources are varied and inexhaustible, while our faith easily drops into a rut and is soon exhausted. Philip's proving, like our own too often, shewed he had been a slow learner in the school of grace. Our Lord had already fed greater multitudes in another wilderness for 40 years, and Philip might have remembered how He brought water out of the flinty rock and gave them bread from heaven to eat, (see eg. Psa 114. 8 and 105. 40) as it is written for his and our learning.

The Lord was "proving" Philip's faith. When Israel murmured and demanded meat for their lust, he should have recalled the Lord's answer, which staggered even Moses, "Ye shall not eat one day, nor two days, nor five days, neither ten days, nor twenty days; but even a whole month" (Num 11 19, 20). How could such an unheard of thing be? "Shall the flocks and the herds be slain for them to suffice them? or shall all the fish of the sea be gathered together for them, to suffice them?" (v 22). Moses could see only two possible ways of feeding with flesh the host of Israel – the slaughter of all their cattle, or a mighty haul of Red Sea fish; but the Lord could see a third and better way. It was to be His provision, not theirs, and He would bring it to their very tents. The Lord knew "what He would do." (John 6. 6). "Is the Lord's hand waxed short? Thou shalt see now whether my word shall come to pass unto thee or not." (Num 11. 23). "The people asked and He brought quails." (Psa 105. 40). But was this in reality a blessing? No. "He gave them their request, but sent leanness into their souls." (Psa 106. 15). A fat body, may hold a lean soul. To the aged who dwell in the house of the Lord it is promised, "They shall be fat and flourishing" (Psa 92. 14).

Jehovah could supply Elijah's needs through the unclean birds of prey, the starving widow in the far-off land of Jezebel, and later in the wilderness, where there were neither ravens nor widows. Once more, "man did eat angels' food," (Psa 78. 25) or at least food from an angel's hand. Deserts are favoured spots for the people of God. It is there they really learn His resources. Elims are preceded by Marahs.

How could famine-stricken Samaria hope for enough and to spare, on the morrow? Unbelief could only suggest one way, and that for it an impossibility. "If the Lord would make windows in heaven, might this thing be?" (2 Kings 7. 2). The Lord might have done it that way. He promises, in fact, to His people, as we know, that if they bring all the tithes into the storehouse – that is the portion of His poor and of His servants – "*to open the windows of heaven* and pour them out such a blessing that there shall not be room enough to receive it" (Mal 3. 10). This blessing is not only spiritual but material, as the following verses show. You may save in doctors' bills and dentists' bills, and bills for repairs, what you have given to the Lord. But to go back to Samaria, was the Lord's hand shortened? Was He shut up to one way of supply? Nay, "He Himself knew what He would do." He made His enemies hear a dreadful sound, and disgorge their rich spoil into the laps of His people. Unbelief did not partake, however, for though it cannot shut up His tender mercies, it can shut off its own share of them. But "God is faithful."

> He knows, He loves, He cares.
> Nothing this truth can dim;
> He always does the best for those,
> Who leave the choice to Him.

"He Himself knew what He would do." So far the apostle ought to have been assured, for He was the Christ – the Power of God and the Wisdom of God; but they could not have guessed how He would provide, for "His ways are past finding out" (Rom 11. 33), and His wisdom is very variegated[1] (Eph 3. 10).

> Deep in unfathomable mines
> Of never-failing skill,
> He treasures up His bright designs,
> And works His sovereign will.

No one would have supposed that this lad, with his little store, would be the source of supply for all this people. Yet he was the providential provision of the Father. God does use means, but very inadequate, save to the eye of faith. "A small round thing, as small as the hoar frost on the ground," (Ex 16. 14) was to nourish the thousands of Israel; the scrapings of a meal barrel; the dregs of a cruse of oil to keep an Elijah alive; three hundred feeble men with trumpets, to deliver His people from a vast host; a little maid to bring Naaman to himself; "the foolishness of preaching to save them that believe." (1 Cor 1. 21). And here no baker's storehouse, but five barley cakes; no great haul, but two insignificant fishes, "weak things" (1 Cor 1. 27) indeed, but "mighty through God." (2 Cor 10. 4). The lad may have been an apostle's boy. He must at least have been of the apostolic band, for in all the other Gospels the apostles speak of the food as being their own. "We have . . .

---

[1] "Polupoikilos" – primarily, marked with a great variety of colours, of cloth, or a painting, then manifesting itself in a great variety of forms, as here.

five loaves and two fishes." (Matt 14. 17). Whoever He was, he was ready at hand at God's moment, and though the supply was meagre, it was enough and to spare, when brought to Christ. Nothing is too small to yield to Him, or too great to withhold. It may remind us of the "deep poverty" of the churches of Macedonia, which, by the grace of God, "abounded unto the riches of their liberality," (2 Cor 8. 2) a feeble echo of that wonderful "grace of our Lord Jesus Christ," who, "though He was rich, yet for your sakes He became poor, that ye through His poverty might be rich." (2 Cor 8. 9). And lest we should think this is something quite outside and beyond our experience, the Spirit of God adds – "God is able to make all grace abound towards you; that ye, always having all sufficiency in all things, may abound to every good work." (2 Cor 9. 8). For He who multiplied the five barley cakes and fish still lives, and can "multiply your seed sown and increase the fruits of your righteousness" (2 Cor 9. 10). "Little is much if God be in it." Did ever crumb grow to bigger loaf, or slender store to richer feast?

Now the guests are seated on the thick grass to ensure their comfort, and in hundreds and fifties, to ensure their orderly supply. "They did all eat and were filled," (Matt 14. 20) and the "fishes divided He among them all." (Mark 6. 41). None were neglected, none surfeited, none unsatisfied. So is God's provision in nature, and in grace. Air, water, sun to be had for the taking, and "food for the service of man," free too, in response to the most modest labour, but for the fall, and in spite of the fall, a full supply of grace through the atoning blood of Christ, available for a guilty world and for needy saints. "My God shall supply all your need, according to His riches in glory by Christ Jesus." (Phil 4. 19). God's care is over all His works, but especially toward "the household of faith," (Gal 6. 10). "He careth for you;" (1 Pet 5. 7) your "Father knoweth that ye have need of all these things;" (Matt 6. 32) therefore, "Take no anxious thought," (Matt 6. 31 (Newberry)). "Be careful for nothing" (Phil 4. 6). "Casting all your care upon Him." (1 Pet 5.7).

Thus the Lord interprets the Father. He provides for the multitude, but He does not forget His own. To each fell a basket of fragments. Surely not half-chewed, mauled pieces of bread and fish. The Lord would not offer such fragments to His servants, but, as I take it, what remained of the great store, "over and above to them that had eaten," (John 6. 13) "good measure pressed down, and shaken together, and running over." (Luke 6. 38). Whatever others may think will do for the Lord's servants, it would not be His thought to provide them other than with something clean, and fresh, and "worthy of God." Had there been thirteen apostles, no doubt there would have been thirteen basketsful. Like the widow's oil, the fragments would not have stayed, when there was another basket to fill. There ought, indeed, to have been a thirteenth basket for the Lord Himself, but He did not lay up in store for His own needs. That, no doubt, it was the privilege of others to do for Him. Thus their individual needs were fully met. Here the word for basket is *kophinos*, a wicker-basket as always in the account of the miracle. But in the account of the feeding of the 4000, another kind of basket – *spuris* –woven out of reeds, is mentioned. There were only seven of these, representing perhaps fulness of supply according to their collective need. Some make much of the individual need, some much of the collective, but both have their important place. No doubt the assembly is made up of individuals, and if the whole is to prosper, it must be through the individual members. But there is also a collective need and responsibility. What may meet the individual need, may not be suitable for the collective. There are the twelve baskets that each may enjoy his individual supply. There are the seven baskets, that no one may say to his brother, "I have no need of thee." (1 Cor 12. 21). We cannot get on alone. We are members of a body, to which every joint supplies its measure.

The feeding of the five thousand evoked a true, though inadequate, acknowledgement to our Lord's Person, "This is of a truth that prophet that should come into the world." (John 6. 14). The remembrance of analogous miracles in the days of Moses and Elisha would enable the multitude, without much spiritual apprehension, to recognise in Him "the prophet" foretold by Moses (Deut 18. 15). According to Dr Edersheim, this prophecy was not held to be Messianic by the ancient Rabbis, which explains the distinction between "Christ" and "that prophet", drawn by the deputation sent by the Pharisees to John the Baptist (John 1. 20, 21). This is used by Moslem controversialists to prove that Jesus was not "that prophet" – a role reserved for Mahomet. But whatever they or the Rabbis may say, our Lord was recognised as "the prophet," not only here, but in Matt 21. 11, where the words should be rendered, "This is the prophet, Jesus, from Nazareth of Galilee." Peter too, by the Spirit, applies the Deuteronomy passage directly to the Lord in Acts 3. 22.

That He, however, was "the Son," "the Heir," did not enter into their conception of things. That He was "come to seek and to save that which was lost," (Luke 19. 10) and that this entailed the work of redemption, met no need of theirs. They would have taken "Him by force, to make Him a King," (John 6.15) but not on His terms – that of repentance, which was the very condition of the Kingdom. Our Lord's refusal to be made a king after man's heart, is no proof He did not come to be their King after God's heart. In His public entry into Jerusalem He had this definite object in view. It was understood in this sense by the multitude of His disciples (quite a distinct class from "the multitude" here), and was so interpreted by the Holy Spirit. "All this was done, that it might be fulfilled, which was spoken by the prophet, saying, 'Tell ye the daughter of Sion, Behold thy King cometh unto thee' " (Matt 21. 4, 5). When the Old Testament prophets speak of "the Kingdom," they refer to the literal Davidic kingdom, based on moral and spiritual sanctions (*eg*, "A King shall reign in righteousness" Isa 32. 1). No refinements of interpretation can explain this away. It is really a serious anachronism to read back into the Jewish prophets the present Gospel dispensation, an interval not then revealed. Israel, as a nation, rejected their King, and are for the present rejected. The Gospel is now proclaimed without distinction to Jew and Gentile, and the old wall of partition is broken down in Christ. To interpret such words as "Behold *thy King* cometh unto thee," as the offer of the Gospel to Israel, as we have it to-day, is to ignore all dispensational truth and introduce serious confusion.

But though the people recognised His miraculous powers for their temporal benefit, and desired to enjoy them further, they had yet a far deeper lesson to learn.

The Lord would interpret the Father, not only as the Supplier of man's material food, but of the Heavenly Bread, the Bread of Life. That would perish with the eating – a temporary provision for a temporal need: this would endure unto "everlasting life," (John 6. 40) increasing as fed upon. That must be earned with the sweat of the brow, this must be believed for. The word for "believe" (v 35) is in the present – "become a believer." But the Lord was in the presence of unbelief, and unbelief has but a short memory, asks for signs and misapplies the Word of the Lord. It was Jehovah, not Moses, who gave the manna to Israel (Neh 9. 15). But at best, that was only the figure of Him who is "the true Bread," (John 6. 32) given by the Father. The bread of earth comes up from the earth, the bread of God (*His* bread before becoming the Bread of life for man), came down from heaven. That sustains life, this gives life unto the world.

Though they asked for the bread, they knew not it was Jesus Himself, nor would they feed on Him, when He gave them to know it. But those given to Christ by the Father, and taught of Him, do come and feed upon the Living Bread with faith and appetite.

The manna could not avert death, but whoso eats this Bread shall never die, but live for ever. But once more, the Heavenly Bread transcends the earthly, for not only does it *give* life, but is itself the "Living Bread." (v 51).

That Bread was His flesh, which He would give for the life of the world. The change of the figure from bread to "flesh" and "blood" (v 53) is very important. There can be no partaking of Christ through incarnation, but only through the death of the Cross, on the ground of accomplished redemption. Those who apply this eating and drinking to partaking of the Lord's supper, under whatever name they term it, fall very far from the truth. The necessity to "eat the flesh and drink the blood" of Christ, as spoken of here, was, and is peremptory and absolute. Achieving that, means eternal life, failing that, eternal death. Who would dare to affirm that everyone partaking of the Lord's supper has eternal life, or omitting to partake is doomed to perish. Moreover, the Lord's supper was not instituted till long after our Lord spoke these words, and yet those addressed were held responsible then and there, to eat His flesh and drink His blood. It is true the Lord had not died, but the types and prophecies were eloquent witnesses to the death of Messiah, the Jews themselves being witnesses. This eating and drinking, is the appropriation of His Person and work. It is a spiritual, not a literal or so-called "sacramental" partaking. "He that hath the Son hath life and he that hath not the Son of God hath not life." (1 John 5. 12). This truth was too hard a saying for many a professed disciple. How could a slain Christ fulfil their hopes of earthly glory? What would they then, were they to see the Son of Man ascend and disappear where He was before, His whole mission to Israel an apparent failure. From that time, many of His disciples went back and walked no more with Him. "Will ye also go away?" (v 67) asked the Lord of the apostles. "Lord, to whom shall we go?" replied Peter, "Thou hast the words of eternal life, and we believe and are sure that Thou art that Christ, the Son of the living God." (v 69). Had he never learnt that lesson before, he had learnt it the previous night when, sinking beneath the waves of the Sea of Galilee, he had felt the strong right hand of Christ grasp and save him. He had tasted that the Lord was gracious. He would learn to feed upon Him still, and in doing so to be conformed daily to His image.

> Man earthy of the earth, an-hungered, feeds
>   On earth's dark poison tree,
> Wild gourds and deadly roots and bitter weeds,
>   And as his food is he.
> And hungry souls there are, that find and eat
>   God's manna day by day,
> And glad they are, their life is fresh and sweet,
>   For as their food are they.

6

IN A SCENE OF "CONTRADICTION"

THE apostle exhorted the Hebrew believers, "Consider Him that endured such contradiction[1] of sinners against Himself, lest ye be wearied and faint in your minds." (Heb 12. 3). The most weighty authorities have here "against themselves," as though the "contradiction" carried with it its

---

[1] The word for "contradiction" is translated sometimes "gainsaying," that is "against-saying," eg, "the gainsaying of Core."

own condemnation, and reacted against the contradictors, as no doubt it did. Certainly the purpose of His coming "to seek and to save," (Luke 19. 10) and the character of His life, going "about doing good," (Acts 10. 38) should have ensured Him a welcome everywhere. The reverse proved how "lost" men were. Thirty years of perfect life did not induce "His brethren" to believe on Him. Were Christians more like Christ in life and testimony, the world, we are told, would treat them right royally; in reality it would treat them more like their Master. His holiness only served to bring out their unholiness; His testimony, their hatred. It is at Jerusalem that this "contradiction" was most marked, and it is John who chiefly presents our Lord's ministry there. Nowhere does the moral glory of the Lord shine more brightly than in this Gospel; nowhere is the hatred of man more manifest. Indeed, John begins as we have before remarked, with rejection, "The light shineth in darkness, and the darkness comprehendeth it not," (John 1. 5) man in his love of sin, "having the understanding darkened." (Eph 4. 18). Again, "He was in the world and the world was made by Him, and the world knew Him not," (John 1. 10) man in his ignorance, "alienated from the life of God, through the ignorance that is in them" (Eph 4. 18) and then "He came unto His own (*idia* – His own things according to the Levitical order, priesthood – temple – sacrifice) but His own (*idioi* – His own people) received Him not." (John 1. 11). "Only man is vile" – and especially religious man – blinded by "the god of this world." (2 Cor 4. 4). But (and here comes in the blessed contrast which grace makes), "As many as received Him to them gave He power to become the sons of God." (John 1. 12).

The greater part of John's Gospel is taken up with the visits of our Lord to Jerusalem, on the occasion of the annual feasts – (1) chaps 2. 13; 3. 21, for the first passover; (2) chap 5, feast not specified; (3) chap 7, for the feast of tabernacles; then (4) chap 10. 22-39, two months later in the ninth month (Chisleu), at the feast of the dedication; and lastly (5) chap 12. 20, for the last Passover.

In **John 2,** the Lord, as the obedient Servant "made under the law," (Gal 4. 4) comes up to Jerusalem for the Passover. If leaven must be put away out from all houses in Israel (Exod 12. 15), how much more from the Father's house? There, judgment must begin; His holiness must be vindicated. The Father will not share His temple with Mammon. The zeal of the perfect Servant, interprets the Father's holy claims. He would restore that which He took not away – even the glory of the Father's house (Psa 69. 5, 9). But His right to do so is challenged by the religious world. They demand a sign. He offers what is virtually the "sign of the prophet Jonas." (Matt 16. 4). There was another "temple" of God, (John 2. 19) which they could not defile, but might destroy. He would raise it up in three days. Hitherto the word for temple has been "*hieron,*" the sacred enclosure. Here, the Lord uses another word, "*naos,*" the inner shrine. The raising up of this "holy temple" would introduce that new order of things, of which He speaks to the woman of Samaria. As she is outside the ordinary channels of His Kingdom ministry, He passes in silence over the true condition of the temple at Jerusalem. It was not for her to know this. It was still the Father's house, though defiled by covetousness. How often has this principle been forgotten by elders or parents, in detailing the failures of "the House of God," before those young in years, or the faith. Little wonder if the tender consciences of such have been stumbled or defiled, and their feet taught to run in other paths than the "ways which be in Christ." (1 Cor 4. 17). The temple at Jerusalem was to be superseded by yet another "House," in which the true worshippers should worship the Father in spirit and in truth. That House would be a temple in which every one doth "speak of His glory" (Psa 29. 9), because every stone is a living worshipper, redeemed with precious blood. Already were

131

some of these stones gathered out to Him, who was to be its Foundation and chief Cornerstone. Is the responsibility any less to-day, to put away leaven, and not to defile the temple of the Holy Spirit? "If any man defile the temple of God, him shall God destroy (defile m)" (1 Cor 3. 17; 5. 8).

Three things characterize "religious" people as a class – attachment to sacred buildings, observance of holy days, and ignorance of the grace of God. All these marked the Jews of our Lord's day. We have seen how His own words in chap 2. were misinterpreted, as derogatory to the Temple. How could He rebuild in three days what thousands had toiled forty-six years to build? Truly He was greater than the Temple, though He did not say so here. These words were never forgotten till the day of His trial before Caiaphas. To-day, to hint that religious buildings of bricks and mortar are in no sense "churches," or "houses of God," but that to form such, "living stones" are needed (1 Pet 2. 5), gives great offence. Here, in **John 5,** the observance of the Sabbath is in question. They would slay "the Lord of the Sabbath" for doing good on His own day. His answer in effect was, The Father is not keeping Sabbath, nor is the Son either. "My Father worketh hitherto, and I work." (John 5. 17). This dates from Eden, when sin broke in on creation rest – the first Sabbath. How could God rest in the presence of sin? Then the Father began to work to recover man from the effects of the transgression, and continued down the ages toward patriarchs, Israel, and the nations, to the very ministry of Christ. In all this, the Son bore His part. "And I work," not only in Divine unison with the Father, but as the Interpreter and Executor of His purposes. Such a statement only fanned their murderous fury. It was an unmistakeable claim to equality with God. That our Lord did not deny, but accepted the inference, is a sufficient answer, among many other such, to the Sadducees of our day, who deny that our Lord ever claimed to be more than a mere man like ourselves. Such a statement can only bespeak Egyptian darkness as to His teachings, or a Satanic malignity against His Person, which refuses the plainest evidence. However, we may "possess our souls in patience." Modernists cannot dethrone the Christ of God – the Divine Son – with their petty negations. So our Lord accepts their inference, but while doing so reveals Himself as the dependent One. "The Son can do nothing of Himself, but what He seeth the Father do." (John 5. 19). As the visible works of creation make manifest the invisible things of the Creator, so the visible works of the Son reflect the invisible things of the Father – His grace, His truth, His love, and that completely and faithfully. "What things soever He doeth, these also doeth the Son likewise," (John 5. 19) withholding nothing, interpolating nothing. This perfect exchange of fellowship, denoting **the essential equality of being of the Son with the Father** is shown in at least seven ways in this chapter.

(1) **In the result of the Father's love** (v 20), the communication of all things to the Son. Perfect love has no secrets, and no reserves (chap 3. 35).

(2) **In the possession by Him of resurrection power** (v 21), in exactly the same way as the Father possesses it. The same voice that now raises dead souls will one day raise "all that are in the graves," (v 28) a general description of those who have died, in whatever way their bodies have been disposed of, whether by burial, cremation, etc. – the saints first, for the resurrection of life, the wicked a millennium later – for the resurrection of judgment (Rev 20. 5-12).

(3) **In the bestowal of the right of judgment** (v 22), supreme recognition of His omniscience and omnipotence. Divine attributes essential to one who would exercise universal judgment.

(4) **In the honours paid** (v 23). Equal honour is to be ascribed to the Son as to the Father. All honour, not equally paid to the Son, is refused by the Father (v 23). With this we may compare 1 John 2. 23, "Whosoever denieth the Son,

the same hath not the Father; he that acknowledgeth the Son hath the Father also." It is of interest to note, that the latter part of the verse has been restored to the text by RV, on overwhelming authority. Modernists and Unitarians, in denying the Son, are altogether "without God" (*atheoi*, Eph 2. 12). They speak of a god and father, "the God of Jesus," but he is an altogether different person to "the God and Father of our Lord Jesus Christ" (*cf.* John 8. 44; 2. Cor 4. 4).

(5) **In the authority of the Word** (v 24). – The Word of the Son is equivalent to the revelation of the Father, and communicates to him who hears and believes it, eternal life, etc.

(6) **In the essential possession of life** (v 26). – This explains the life-conveying voice of the Son. He has life in Himself. This is much more than merely "having life" just as "alone having immortality" (1 Tim 6. 16m) is far greater than merely "being immortal." For if only God be immortal, then we must deny immortality even to the "elect angels" and to believers, whereas it is the property of all God's moral creatures. The living believer will put on *bodily* immortality when the Lord returns (1 Cor 15. 53). He, in common with all men and angels, has immortality in His spiritual nature as a derived gift. God only possesses it inherently. This is the essential attribute of Him who, "in the beginning, was the Word" (John 1. 1).

(7) **In the power to execute judgment** (v 27). – Not only to pass sentence, as above (3), but to carry it into effect. One who is truly man is to execute judgment on man. But even in this, the Lord disclaims independence of the Father. All His judgments will interpret the Father's will (v 20). Nor is His witness merely personal. He can cite as witness John, "that burning and shining light," (v 35) and greater witness still, the works the Father had given Him to do, nay, the Father Himself and the Holy Scriptures, which they professed to honour. All bore testimony that He had come

from the Father. But how could His enemies believe this testimony while receiving honour one of another? No doubt the same tendency is a hindrance to faith to-day. May we rather seek the honour that cometh from God only!

The lying accusation of violating the Sabbath, followed the Lord with a threat on His life. So as **John 7** records He "walked in Galilee, for He would not walk in Jewry, because the Jews sought to kill Him" (v 1). There seems an intimate and inherent connection between lies and murder. The liar is a potential murderer. He who would slay the truth, would slay all else. The devil, the Lord tells us, "was a murderer from the beginning (*i.e.,* of his fall), and abode not in the truth" (chap 8. 44), as though the two sins synchronised. He became a murderer, the moment he departed from the truth. The first man born in the world was, as we know, a liar and a murderer. Sin was born full-grown. In the first sin, every sin existed in embryo.

Because the Lord was "delivered by the determinate counsel and foreknowledge of God," some would condone the guilt of man at the Cross. But the Spirit testifies that the hands that slew Him were "wicked hands" (Acts 2. 23). We know from the Gospels how often before, they would have slain Him, but His hour was not yet come (John 7. 20). It was not the will, but the power they lacked. But everything must be done in the Father's time, even as to going up to the Feast of Tabernacles. To Him, "made under the law" (Gal 4. 4), this was a direct call, but *when* to go was in the Father's hand. His brethren knew nothing of the Father's will, or the Father's time. Personal choice and policy alone entered into their conception of things. But with the Lord it was far otherwise: He did the Father's will, at the Father's call.

"Known unto God are all His works from the beginning of the world" (Acts 15. 18), and also the moment of their accomplishment. It was "when *the fulness of the time* was come, that God sent forth His Son" (Gal 4. 4), not a moment too soon, nor a moment late. *"In due time,* Christ died for the ungodly" (Rom 5. 6), and also *"in due time"* God will exalt those who humble themselves under His mighty hand (1 Pet 5. 6).

> Rest in the Lord and wait for Him;
>   But wait thou with a patient mind;
> God never hastes before His time,
>   Nor doth He ever lag behind.

It was only when His brethren had gone up, that God's hour struck for Him to go also, and half the feast had passed ("lost time," the carnal would say) e'er the moment arrived for him to go up to the temple to teach. In these days of hustle and hurry and multiple "engagements" and of "bookings up" months and sometimes years ahead, of precipitate decisions and of "cut and dried" arrangements, do we not need to be solemnly reminded of the possibility of doing the right thing at the wrong time, or the wrong thing with possibly the right motive? It is to be feared that with many, there is not that continued "waiting upon" God, that once was known among those who serve. Instead of enquiring His mind, we "make up *our* minds," and then pray for God's blessing. Instead of following the Lamb whithersoever He goeth, we too often ask Him to follow us.

> But Jesus followeth not, He only leads.

The result is, we often sow much and bring in little; we eat but we have not enough (see Hag 1. 6).

To return to our Lord in the temple. Such teaching could only call forth the wonder of the Jews. How could one not "of the schools" teach thus? "My doctrine is not Mine, but His that sent Me," (v 16) was the reply; "if any man will do His will, he shall know of the doctrine, whether it be of God or whether I speak from Myself." (v 17). "He that speaketh from himself (that is, out of his own head, on his own initiative), seeketh his own glory; but he that seeketh His glory that sent him, (by only speaking His message) the same is true, and no unrighteousness is in him." (v 18). The Lord thus disclaimed all originality in His teachings. They were the words of the Father, of which He was the mouthpiece. He was the interpreter of Divine words, inaudible to all but Himself. He spake the Word of God in the very words of God. No wonder unprejudiced men, even officially His enemies, testified, "Never man spake like this man" (chap 7. 46). We do not remember such a testimony being ever rendered to any of the "modern critics" even by their own friends. And yet they presume to criticise our Lord, and talk of their own superior attainments and "scholarship." We can imagine someone saying of them. "Never man boasted like these men." But though the Lord spake only the Words of God, the Father delighted to reveal Him and so gave Him to testify of Himself. "If any man thirst, let him come unto Me and drink." (v 37). "I am the light of the world; he that followeth Me shall not walk in darkness, but shall have the light of life." (John 8. 12). He speaks of Himself and of the Father in one breath, "I and the Father that sent Me." (John 8. 16). "If ye had known Me, ye should have known My Father also" (John 8. 19) and of His pre-existence, "Before Abraham was, I am" (John 8. 58). Could any mere man nourish such astounding pretensions? Would He not shock the confidence even of His disciples? And yet our Lord in making these transcendent claims, is not challenged by His critics to-day on the ground of vanity, or even of a lack of sobriety.

7

IN A SCENE OF MOURNING (*John 11*)

WE have already seen our Lord at Cana, in the house of feasting. We are now to see Him interpreting the Father in the house of mourning. There "He rejoices with them that do rejoice," here, He "weeps with them that weep." (see Rom 12. 15). "It is better," the Preacher tells us, "to go to the house of mourning than to the house of feasting, for that is the end of all men, and the living will lay it to heart." And "the heart of the wise is in the house of mourning, but the heart of fools in the house of mirth" (Eccl 7. 2, 4). The world's feasts must sooner or later turn to mourning, and that often very suddenly. "Their laughter is like the crackling of thorns under a pot," but for a moment. But who but Christ can turn the house of mourning into a house of feasting? This is what we see at Bethany. The Comforter of chap 11 becomes the Guest of chap 12. "There they made Him a supper," (v 2) and the mourners of yesterday serve and adore. Thus will it be for every Christian mourner. "Weeping may endure for a night, but joy cometh in the morning" (Psa 30. 5). "Blessed are they that mourn, for they shall be comforted" (Matt 5. 4). "God shall wipe away all tears from their eyes" (Rev 21. 4).

The sisters of Bethany knew to whom to turn in their sorrow. "A brother is born for adversity," (Prov 17. 17) but their brother was sick unto death. They knew the "Friend that sticketh closer than a brother." (Prov 18. 24). They had received Him into their house, He had supped with them and where He sups, He sympathises too. They were so sure of His readiness to come to their help, they had but to mention the need. "Lord, behold he whom Thou lovest, is sick." (v 3). The word here for love, *Philein,* is not as weighty as that used in verse 5, *Agapan.* Though in a sense it is *strong,* it is not so *deep. Philein* implies a more passionate warmth of affection, but *Agapan* a love of more reasoned, deliberate choice. *Philein* knows to the full, how well it loves; *Agapan* can tell you why it loves. Yes, the Lord did love with the love of special friendship, and thus only displayed the perfection of His true humanity. But it was without prejudice to the fact that He loved all His disciples. No doubt John was one of His special friends, as were the three mentioned here. Those who insist on our Lord's Deity (and thank God for all such!), must not do so at the expense of His true Humanity, or they seriously err from the faith, and disparage the glory of His Person. Abraham and Moses were "friends of God," and no doubt the capacity for such friendship was originally one of the beautiful qualities of unfallen humanity, and now is restored in part to believers. Should we not expect to find it in fullest measure in the Perfect Man? The command to love all the brethren, does not mean by making all our special friends. For to "love" and to "*like*" are not the same. The latter term implies a certain similarity of tastes, disposition, and ways. When the Lord received the message of His friends at Bethany. He "abode two days still in the place where He was." (v 6). This delay may throw light on mysteries that cross our own path, unexplained trials, apparently fruitless prayers, permissions of God's providence, that seem to lend themselves to misunderstandings. "Thy way is in the sea, and Thy path in the great waters, and Thy footsteps are not known" (Psa 77. 19), and by man cannot be, save in "the sanctuary of God" (Psa 73. 17). So the Lord says, "What I do thou knowest not *now*; but thou shalt know hereafter" (John 13. 7).

The Lord might have saved Lazarus from dying, as He had the nobleman's son (chap 4. 50), and the centurion's servant (Matt 8. 13), but here things must be allowed to go to the very worst. To save him "out of death" would be the greater deliverance. Nature says, "While there is life there is hope," and the sisters could not then see further than that, but faith must learn that "while there is Christ there is hope." There is for us all in trial, a bigger question even than "*How* to get out of it?" and that is, "*What* to get out of it?"

Another reason for the delay, which is sometimes overlooked, was that the Lord knew that, travelling at the ordinary pace of men, He and His disciples would have arrived too late, even had they started to Bethany without delay. His failure to arrive in time would then have been gloated over by His enemies of to-day as a proof He possessed no real claim to omniscience. As it was, there was no haste, no hurry, and when they arrived, after a delay of only two days, they found Lazarus had been in the grave "four days already." (v 17). Indeed, e'er our Lord started on His journey, He knew that His friend was already dead. But when He arrives, He brings present deliverance. As in the case of Jairus' daughter and the widow's son, so here. There was no need for Martha to wait for "the resurrection at the last day." (v 24). The very Son of God, whose voice will then wake the dead, was present in all His resurrection power. So He said, "I am the Resurrection and the Life; he that believeth in Me, though he were dead, yet shall he live; and whosoever liveth and believeth in Me, shall never die." (vv 25-26). These words seem to rise prophetically far above that dispensation. The mystery of the coming of the Lord to raise the dead and change the living (1 Cor 15.; 1 Thess 4. 15) had not then been unfolded. Yet we see it enfolded in these words of our Lord, to Martha. To those who vainly seek to find opposition between the teachings of the apostle Paul and His Master, and whose parrot and, we fear, hypocritical cry is, "Back to Christ," to escape "the pricks" of apostolic doctrine, we reply, there is not a truth found in the Epistles, that was not already *latent* in our Lord's teaching. Both are equally the fruit of "the Holy Spirit's teaching." Now, the Lord is about to display His power over death, as the Son of God. Will this hinder the deep outflow of His tender compassions as Son of Man, towards the mourners in their sorrow? No, indeed. In His groaning – for "He groaned in the spirit" (v 33) – we hear the beating of the heart of God.

In the trouble of soul which the Lord manifested at the sorrow of those whom He loved – for "He troubled Himself" (v 33, marg.) – we learn the practical workings of the Divine sympathies. In His tears – for "Jesus wept" (v 35) – we behold the tender mercies of our God. Whoever else may be indifferent to the sorrows of His people, it certainly is not He. For truly, "in all their affliction He was afflicted." (Isa 63. 9). It is a fact, that may well arrest our thoughts, that we have in this scene, not merely the display of Divine power in the raising of Lazarus, wonderful though that be, but in the expression of His sympathy with the sorrow that death had wrought, we learn the affections of Him, of whom He was "the express image," (Heb 1. 3) "the Father of Mercies, and the God of all Comfort." (2 Cor 1. 3). Not only then were the sisters comforted by the Lord's real human sympathy, but in God's time and way, their prayer was granted by His Divine power. This was, as God loves to answer, in a better way than they asked or thought. They received their brother back, not from a dying bed, but from the tomb. But would not the other have been better? How much anguish it would have spared them! Yes, but what lessons they would have missed! What are usually called "wonderful answers" to prayer, are those received with the least possible delay, and in striking coincidence with the request. Such are certainly very blessed, and call for heartfelt praise. But often more wonderful still are the prayers answered in God's better time and way. The answers we *insist* on, may prove anything but blessings in disguise, and ensue in leanness of soul. Hezekiah's added 15 years (2 Kings 20. 6) saw his failure before the King of

Babylon (v 12), the birth of Manasseh (chap 21. 1, 2), and only one act which the Spirit of God has seen fit to leave for our instruction: "He made a pool and conduit and brought water into the city" (chap 20. 20), a record of service much below the level of those first fruitful years of his reign, his originally alloted span.

Cases are not unknown to-day of lives prolonged in answer to insistent prayer, which have wasted out in backsliding and dishonour to the Lord. The Lord's people may always count on His tender sympathy as they minister at a sick bed, but even when restoration is withheld, they can await a better answer, on the resurrection morn. The Lord was summoned once, we know, to another house of mourning, but here there was no delay in His response, for, as far as we know, Jairus was not a disciple, and what faith he had was only in the bud, and must not be nipped, as had been the case had "Jesus abode still in the place where He was." The delay caused by the healing of the sick woman, was no doubt providentially permitted to allow things to get beyond the hope of man. Trying, no doubt, was the crisis, but it elicited those four cheering words, "Fear not, only believe" (Mark 5. 31), which we may well cherish. Here (Mark 5) the Lord found the house full of the world's mourners, well-meaning persons enough, but representing that official unbelief which would sooner see the dead girl buried "decently and in order," than raised from her bed by any unorthodox methods. Then let them go bag and baggage, with their commonsense unbelief, and only those remain worth training in the ways of God, or whose spark of faith may thus be fanned into a flame! Let *these* "see the goodness of the Lord in the land of the living"; (Psa 27. 13) the others counted not, for they were very blind. This incident forms the link between the raising of Lazarus and that of the son of the widow of Nain (Luke 7. 12). Here, there was no request to the Lord for help. Neither was the miracle done in private, like the last. "Many of His disciples went with Him and much people," (v 11) and they met the crowded funeral procession – the widowed mother and "much people of the city was with her" (v 12). One would judge she was a person beloved, and of some position in the city. It was the most public occasion possible. The Lord manifested forth His glory before many witnesses. The widow made no appeal to Him, as Jairus or the sisters of Bethany; but he could not be indifferent in the presence of her tears. "And when the Lord saw her, He had compassion on her, and said unto her, Weep not," (v 13) thus once more interpreting the heart of Him whose "tender mercies are over all His works." (Psa 145. 9). Then He gave life to the dead, and delivered him to his mother, perhaps in such a case the only practical way of drying her tears. We do not see the dead raised to-day. These miracles are now in abeyance. But a miracle of miracles is still to take place at the return of "this same Jesus." (Acts 1. 11). The dead in Christ shall rise first, the living in Christ shall be changed, and both together caught up to meet the Lord in the air, and so shall we ever be with the Lord (see 1 Thess 4. 16-18). This is the Divine consolation to-day for believers, mourning the loss of their fellow-saints. "Wherefore comfort one another with these words."

8

IN THE MIDST OF HIS OWN (John 13)

OUR Lord's farewell discourse must always hold a peculiar place in the hearts of His people. He was about "to depart out of this world unto the Father," (John 13.1) and that by the way of Golgotha. But, "having loved His own which were in the world, He loved them unto the end," (v 1). He was more occupied with their troubles, needs, and fears, than with His own sorrows. And even the great episode of His passion is hardly alluded to, except indirectly, as a passing interlude – "A little while and ye shall not see Me; (while He lay in the tomb), and again, a little while, and ye shall see Me, (during the subsequent forty days), because I go to the Father," (John 16. 16). How does He provide for the needs of those He was leaving? He reveals to them the Father's Name, and commits them to the Father's care.

All last farewells are touching, and memorable. We see things then in their true relation. Hence we treasure parting words, and respect last wishes. How much more when great spiritual truths are involved, and it is the Lord who is saying farewell! The farewells of Scripture would form a profitable study. Those of Jacob, Moses, Paul, contain important teachings, but our Lord's parting words of grace and truth transcend them all. Like Ezekiel's river, healing and life-giving, they deepen as they flow, and become "waters to swim in, a river that could not be passed over" (Ezek. 47. 5). Jacob and Moses spoke as men about to die, our Lord as one about to pass into the realms of life eternal. The thought of death is bridged; ascension alone is in view. He was going to God, "to the Father," to Him that sent Him.

Chapter 13 is introductory, and divides itself into three sections.

a. The washing of the bathed ones (vv 1-17).
b. The elimination of the unbathed one (vv 18-30).
c. The comfort of the cleansed ones (ver 31, and on intö chap 14).

Feet-washing at meal time, was a common eastern custom. The disciples knew it must be done. But who was to do it? Some post of honour they would have filled, but such a menial service could bring no credit. Perhaps Peter hoped John would do it; Thomas, Philip. Why should not James the less? that other James would say to himself. "Simon Zelotes, thou hast much 'zeal' for many things, why not for this?" But none moved, and then behold a sight to make the angels wonder and saints blush for themselves, and then adore: the Lord of Glory stooping before twelve failing creatures of the dust, and washing their feet! At Calvary, we see the supreme act of obedience to the Father. Do we not see here, the lowliest act of ministry to man? By the literal act of washing, the Lord shows He really did care for the refreshment and comfort of His disciples, "leaving us an example" (1 Pet 2. 21) that we should follow His steps, as the Phebes, the Marys, and Gaius have done since (Rom 16. 2, 6; 3 John 5, 6). But had that been all, He would not have said to Peter, "What I do thou knowest not now; but thou shalt know hereafter," (v 7). Peter knew well the use of the literal washing, but he did not know the spiritual significance of the act.

Water has three principal meanings in the Word of God.

1. When it **submerges** it signifies judgment, as in the flood, the Red Sea and Jordan. Those "waves and billows" of Psalm 42. 7, those, "deep waters" of Psalm 69 1-2, overwhelming the Holy One, speak of the judgment of Calvary. Man cannot evade judgment. There is only one way to escape out of it, he must pass under it, linked with One who can descend into its deepest depths and emerge again. This in figure the ark (Heb *tehvah*) did at the flood, and the ark (Heb. *ah-rohn*) of the covenant in the swellings of Jordan. There is resurrection for the believer who is identified by faith with Christ in His death, of which identification baptism is a *figure*. But there will be no resurrection from the "baptism of fire," the holy wrath of God, which will overwhelm every sinner out of Christ.

2. When water is used **internally** it stands for the spiritual blessing of the Holy Spirit flowing from a crucified and

risen Christ. "They drank of that spiritual Rock that followed them; and that Rock was Christ," (1 Cor 10. 4). We have the same thought in the gladdening river of Psalm 45, bringing earthly blessings to the City of God, and in the pure river of life clear as crystal of Rev 21 bringing heavenly blessing to a universe of bliss.

3. But when water is applied **externally** it signifies cleansing, and that in two ways: either (a) as the purification from positive defilement through contact with death, *e.g.*, "the water of purification" of Num 19, which has its parallel in the restoration to communion of 1 John 1. 9; or (b) as the cleansing of the ways through the Word of God (see Exod. 30. 18, the washing of the laver). This latter, I judge is in view here.

The Lord was about to enter into the holiest of all. His desire, was, that His disciples should have "part with Him" in this. As far as we know, they were not guilty at the moment of any special sin, but their ways must be brought under the power of the Word, and cleansed thereby (Psa 119. 9). They had already passed through the complete bathing of Lev 8. 6, the initial act in the setting apart of the priests, corresponding to the once for all washing of regeneration, the fruit of faith in Christ. But they needed to be cleansed at the laver, which stood between the altar and the door of the tabernacle proper. "He that is bathed (*louesthai*) needeth not save to wash (*niptesthai*) his feet, but is clean every whit," (v 10m). The washing of regeneration needs no repetition; the washing of renewal needs it constantly.

In verse 13 of our chapter, it is really more emphatic than it is as given in our version – "Ye call Me THE Teacher (*Ho Didaskalos*) and THE Lord." Both these titles Christ accepted, for He it was who had the wisdom to teach the truth, and the authority to command obedience to it. In v 14, He reverses the order of these titles, as though to emphasise a fact very easily forgotten, namely, that the only way really to learn, is to obey – "A good understanding have all they that *do* His commandments" (Psa 11. 10). Let the saints then follow His example, and so wash one anothers' feet. It has been said, "If we want to correct fellow-believers, we must *not* wash their feet in boiling water." That is true. But I doubt if "feet washing" means correction, so much as a ministry of refreshment and edification. If we walked more in the Spirit, we should miss fewer opportunities in visits, at meals, in journeyings, in the interval at conferences, for "edifying one another in love." At a large conference lately, a local brother took my arm during an interval, and asked me to go for a short walk. No address I heard helped me more than that short spell of christian converse. The exchange of thought and christian experience, was truly refreshing, and when I think of the conference, that brother's face comes always first before me. This is better than unprofitable talks on divisions of the past, or dissensions in the present, which bulk so largely, and not always necessarily, in our conversational programme, leaving the heart empty and sad.

But the disciples needed something more than the laver, they needed to be purged as a priestly company, from one who was *with* them, but not *of* them, who could not "show his register" (Ezra 1. 62), who had, in fact, never been "bathed" in the waters of "regeneration," according to the priestly order referred to above. Such an one must as polluted be put from the priesthood. Judas' feet had been washed with the others, but the symbolic meaning was lacking in his case. "Ye are clean, *but not all,*" said the Lord, "for He knew who should betray Him" (vv 10-11) Judas could have no part *with* Him, because he had no part *in* Him. Later, the Lord makes the same exception, "If ye know these things, happy are ye if you *do* them," (v 17). "I speak not of you *all*", (v 18). This may recall His earlier words, "Have not I chosen you twelve, and one *of you* is a devil?" For Jesus knew from the beginning who they were that believed not, and who should betray Him" (John 6. 70, 64). Let us never call the unsaved "clean," or expect the dead to "do these things."

This last verse may serve among many similar passages to make it clear, that when the Lord "emptied Himself" (Phil. 2. 7, RV), it was not of His Divine attributes, but of their independent use. "He emptied Himself," as Dr Lightfoot puts it, "of the insignia of His Majesty," but not of what He personally was. In becoming the bond-servant of the Father, He did not know less as a Divine Person than before. He remembered a past eternity (John 17. 5), and even His human consciousness went back to His birth (Psa 22. 9, 10). He knew all things (John 16. 30). "He knew what was in man, the prerogative of Deity" (see Jer 17. 9, 10). He knew the Father, as the Father knew Him (John 10. 15). This embraces all knowledge,[1] so that we are not surprised that He "knew from the beginning . . . who should betray Him," (John 6. 64). But He did not use this knowledge to expose Judas befor the Father's time. But when that time arrived, He revealed unerringly – yet how painfully to His tender heart – the solemn truth to the unsuspecting disciples in a *crescendo* of unmistakable clearness. "He that eateth bread with Me, hath lifted up his heel *against* Me" (v 18). "One of you shall betray Me" (v 21). "He it is, to whom I shall give a sop, when I have dipped it" (v 26). And then directly to the traitor himself, "That thou doest, do quickly" (v 27). He could not fully teach the disciples of the Father, in the presence of the traitor. The Lord was under constraint till Judas had "gone out" into the night. But now He can speak freely, and uses to them for the first time in His ministry, the endearing name, "Little children," (v 33) He looks beyond the shame of the Cross to His own and His

---

[1] Whatever then Mark 14. 32, "neither the Son," means, it must be taken, not as an isolated passage, but in conjunction with the above passages and many others, in which the omniscience of the Lord, is set forth.

people's glorification, and to the glory that will accrue to God thereby, and to a further glory which He would receive. "God shall *also* glorify Him in Himself," (v 32) and that straightway. We see here how intimately the glory of the Father was bound up in the work of Christ and the glory of Christ. They could not follow Him then, they would later. A parting command He enjoins on them that they love one another, even as He had loved them, and that not for His sake alone, but for the sake of their testimony that the world might know they were His disciples.

Additional note

It may not be out of place here to add a few proofs that the Lord Jesus, in His interpretation of the Father was ever the Man that was His Fellow, His Co-equal, possessing to the full His Divine attributes, and that without prejudice to the fact that He "took upon Him the form of a servant," (Phil 2. 7). While holding fast the true Humanity of the Lord, we must never allow it in the sense of so-called modern teaching, which uses it as a handle to deny His Deity, or while loudly professing to hold that, virtually denies it, by depriving Him of that which is inseparable from it, His Divine attributes.

1. OMNISCIENCE. "Jesus . . . knew all men, and needed not that any should testify of man" (John 2. 24, 25). Again, "Jesus knew from the beginning who they were that believed not, and who should betray Him" (chap 6. 64). And in the end, the disciples were constrainted to confess, "Now are we sure that Thou *knowest all things* . . . by this we believe that Thou camest forth from the Father" (chap 16. 20; *cf.* chap 21. 17). He alone knows the Father absolutely (Matt 2. 27). This could not be were He not in the fullest sense GOD, for none but God can "search the hearts" or know God.

2. OMNIPRESENCE. It is clear tht this attribute of Deity must have been more veiled than the others, but our Lord's own testimony claims this for Himself, *e.g.*, in such expressions as "The only begotten Son which is in the bosom of the Father," or "the Son of Man which is in heaven'" (John 1. 18; 3. 13); though in bodily presence He was in Jerusalem. Certainly no one claims omnipresence for our Lord's body even today. It is on the Throne of God, and certainly on no so-called altar or elsewhere on earth. The Lord's well-known declaration, in connection with the gathering together of His disciples in His Name, involves the possession of this attribute, for how else could He be everywhere in the midst (Matt. 18. 20). And this is no less true of the great missionary promise of Matt 28. 20, "Lo, I am with you *alway*," said the risen Christ to His servants, "even unto the end of the Age." What! Christ *at the same time* with all His servants, in all parts of His great harvest field! Then, He must be God over all; for He owns this attribute which is peculiar to God alone. And all this is true, even though as to His human body, He is now seated on the right hand of the Majesty on high.

3. OMNIPOTENCE. Since our Lord Jesus created and upholds heaven, earth and all things, since He is able to subdue all things unto Himself (Phil 3. 21), and finally, since He is distinctly called *the Almighty* (Rev. 1. 8), it is evident that this glorious attribute, also belongs to Him. The One who possesses these Divine powers cannot be a creature only: He is surely nothing less than Jehovah, equal in wisdom, love, majesty, and power, with the Father, and the Holy Spirit.

Of all the confessions of Christ, recorded in the Gospels, that of Thomas reaches the highest watermark. When fully convinced of the reality of the Lord's resurrection, he looked up into His face and said, "MY LORD AND MY GOD," (John 20. 28). And note well – for the point is important – the Lord Jesus did not disown these titles, nor refuse the homage implied, nor did He rebuke His disciple, for so addressing Him, nor others, on similar occasions in His ministry. Yet, if He had not known Himself to be Supreme God, and had not wished His followers to believe in Him as such, and to honour Him accordingly, He would surely have set them right on such a stupendously important matter. His silent acceptance of these high titles proves, He knew Himself to be IMMANUEL, God with us.

With the scene above referred to, compare another incident preserved for us in Rev 19. 10. In the latter case, our judgment approves of the rebuke administered to John. For the one at whose feet he would have worshipped, was like himself a creature, and a servant of their common Lord. And if Christ were only a creature, although the highest, He too would surely have rebuked those who, at moments of special crises "worshipped Him," *e.g.* (Matt 14. 33; 28. 9, 17), and thus would have robbed God of His Divine rights.

Angels, as well as redeemed sinners, are to worship Him. As it is written, "When He bringeth again the First-Begotten into the world He saith, And let all the angles of God *worship Him*" (Heb 1. 6, RV). In the fulness of time, it will be known that the throne of God and of the Lamb, is one and the same. Nearest to the throne, the Church, composed of redeemed sinners, will find her place. And she will join in a song, peculiar to herself as redeemed and glorified, and other circles too of the redeemed. But outside these circles, angels innumerable are to be seen. And beyond these, shall be gathered a great company composed of "every creature which is in heaven, and on the earth and under the earth, and such as are in the sea, and all that are in them" saying, *"Blessing, and honour, and glory, and power, be unto Him that sitteth upon the throne, and unto the Lamb for ever and ever"* (Rev 5. 8-13).

9

COMFORTING THEM (John 14)

OUR Lord, as we have seen, was about to introduce His disciples in spirit within the veil. His sacerdotal prayer would initiate them into that high priestly intercession, which He was so soon to undertake on their behalf. This would entail His leaving them, for, on the earthly plane, He could not be a priest, being outside that family which, by God's appointment, had the monopoly of priestly service on the earth. He must enter *by* His own blood into the heavenly temple, not made with hands, and there, in the presence of the Father, become a Priest of another order than the earthly, that of Melchizedek, Priest of the Most High God King of Righteousness, and King of Peace. In view, then, of their priestly worship, the disciples needed preparation; in view of His departure, consolation. He loved them so much He could not bear that they should be troubled. "Let not your heart be troubled" (v 1). Later on, while repeating the same exhortation, he adds, "neither let it be afraid" (v 27). They were neither to sorrow for the present, nor fear for the future. Nor were these words of comfort addressed only to some élite of disciples, some favoured inner circle, who by their special faithfulness had merited this reward. No, but to a feeble company, slow to understand, and slower to believe; a self-confident Peter; a doubting Thomas, sons of Baonerges, who had drunk but little into the spirit of their Master; eleven men in fine, who were about to forsake Him in His darkest hour. But at the core their hearts beat true: they were "His own." (13. 1) He loved them, and in their measure they loved Him. And so He would comfort their hearts, and for this bequeathed them His peace. "Peace I leave with you. My peace I give unto you: not as the world giveth, give I unto you," (v 27). Why "not as the world?" The world offers "peace, peace, when there is no peace," reiterates peace! but gives no solid or sufficient grounds for it. As the dying infidel bitterly replied, when his friends urged him to hold on, "I have nothing to hold on to." But the peace Christ gives, is based on facts, His blood, His life, His promises, His faithfulness. His consolations are not mere words; they rest on solid grounds.

The first is, that, though no longer visible, *He would be as real as ever.* "Ye believe in God, believe also in Me." (v 1) God, unseen, was the Object of their faith, so was *He* now to be. Though lost to sight, He would be present to faith. Seeing is believing to the world: to the Christian "faith is . . . the evidence of things not seen," (Heb 11. 1). Another fact to comfort them was, *He would be as busy about them, as He had ever been.* As hitherto He had cared and provided for them, so He would not now forget them. "In My Father's house are many mansions; if it were not so, I would have told you. I go to prepare a place for you," (v 2) and what could eleven homeless men need more than that? Not even those wonderful "mansions in the skies," (Greek, "monai." abiding places; compare in Scotch, "manse.") already existing, would suffice; a special "place" must be prepared. There will be different circles of the elect in heaven, but only one centre, Christ; many mansions for the redeemed of past and future dispensations, but only one "place" for the church. Each member will have his allotted sphere, but all will be together in that one place.

Not only so, but the separation would not be long. *He would soon return.* "And if I go and prepare a place for you, I will come again and receive you unto myself." (v 3) The word is literally "I am coming." As a mother, busy in the kitchen, for her weeping child in the nursery, might calm it by calling, "I'm coming! I'm coming! "so the Lord is ever on the point of coming to summon His saints to meet Him in the air, that where He is, there they may be also. It is not "adieu," but "au revoir."[1] Again, while awaiting their entrance into the Fathers house, *He would introduce them into the Father's presence.* Where He was going literally, He would bring them spiritually. "I am the Way" – the only Way into the Father's presence, "no man cometh unto the Father but by Me." "I am the Truth" – the only revelation of the Father. "He that hath seen Me, hath seen the Father," "I am the Life," the only life suitable to the Father's presence. "Because I live, ye shall live also," (see vv 6-9). Then correspondence is a great resource in separation. *The believer is in correspondence with the Father,* and with his absent Saviour. "Whatsoever ye shall ask in My Name, that will I do, that the Father may be glorified in the Son," (v 13). "If ye shall ask ME[2] anything in My Name I will do it," (v 14). The Lord undertakes to see to it that every communication is answered, whether addressed to Him or the Father. What a resource is this opened to faith! We are brought into intimate touch with the Unseen. Moreover, *the Lord promises them another Comforter.* "I will pray the Father, and He shall give you another Comforter," (v 16) who would never leave them – as He must, but who would abide with them for ever. Thus would they be taught more deeply what they had already learned, and be initiated into fresh truths concerning their absent Lord. Indeed, in that Spirit He would Himself come, and not leave them orphans, and in that day they would know that He was in the Father and the Father in Him, and He in them.

One more comfort was theirs. "Ye have heard how I said unto you, I go away, and come again unto you. *If ye loved*

---

[1] In French, "adieu" is rarely if ever, used for saying "good-bye," for this has the sense of a definite separation, but "au revoir," which looks forward to meeting again, and that soon.

[2] The RV inserts "me" on the authority of the two oldest MSS, and this avoids what otherwise might seem a repetition in these two verses.

Me ye would rejoice, because I said I go unto the Father; for My
Father is greater than I." (v 28). His atoning work
accomplished, He would enter into His rest and reward.
The Man of Sorrows would be anointed with the oil of joy
above His fellows. It would comfort their hearts to know,
that for Him at least, was "passed the dark and dreary
night."

10

TEACHING THEM (John 15)

TO be familiar with a river, through daily crossing its ferry,
is different from exploring its reaches, and even then what
goes on below the surface – the life of the river – remains
unknown. The latter only, in a small degree, is perceived by
fishermen or divers. So with the Scriptures. It is good to
cross and recross them, to explore them from Genesis to
Revelation, but it is by penetrating beneath their suface that
we really become familiar with their teaching. John, chapter
15 is a case in point. May the Spirit lead us deeper into its
blessed reality and experience.

There is an evident break between chapters 14 and 15. At
this point the Lord leads His disciples from the lighted
guest-chamber into the dark night, along the way to
Gethsemane. His discourse undergoes a corresponding
change. Till then, it had spoken of consolation in view of
His speedy departure; now it takes on a tone of exhortation
and warning. The disciples were being left behind in a
wilderness – barren and hostile. Could they bear fruit in
such unpropitious soil? The Lord's opening words supply
the answer. He appears to them in a new character, "I am
the true Vine," and "The Father" is revealed in a new

relationship: "And My Father is the Husbandman," (v 1). The great secret is out. The Lord is not only the Messiah of Israel, the Light, the Bread of Life, the Door, the Resurrection and the Life, the Way, but He is also the only Source of fruitfulness. This surely brings the disciples very near to their Lord, for He goes on to say, "Ye are the branches," (v 5) and the Father as Husbandman very near to the disciples; for there is not a branch in this Vine, He does not tend.

Before further considering the teaching of the chapter, we will refer to two other vines of Scripture – the vine of Israel, and the vine of the earth. In the great prophetic chapter of Rev 14, three ingatherings are presented: the presentation of the firstfruits[1], the 144,000 of Israel; the harvest of the earth, probably the fruit of their testimony; and the vintage of the earth – the judgment of God on the vine of the earth. In this last symbol we have a figure of a man as left to himself, under the leadership of Satan's two men, the Man of Sin and the Antichrist, man, that is, at his worst. Would such a vine produce fruit acceptable to God? Clearly not. Could not then man at his best do so? The national history of Israel, is the answer. She was "the vine brought out of Egypt", favoured with every privilege, and tended with every care. But for fruit, she brought forth "wild grapes" (see Psa 80. 8-19; Isa 5. 4). This culminated in the rejection of God's well beloved Son. "This is the Heir: come let us kill him, that the inheritance shall be our's," (Luke 20. 14). Thus man at his best, turned out to be like man at his worst, unable to bring forth any real fruit for God. But when man fails, as he always does in responsibility; God has already provided a resource in the Son of Man, whom He made strong for Himself (see Psa 80. 17), "the true Vine," whose branches, like Joseph's the

---

[1] This evidently corresponds with the wheat harvest. Christ is the fistfruits of the former harvest, in which the Church will be garnered in, corresponding to the barley ingathering.

fruitful bough, ran "over the wall" (Gen 49. 22), in His case of heaven. Christ is the only source of fruit to God, and of blessing to man. As the prophet says, "From ME is thy fruit found" (Hos 14. 8).

The vine is surely a wonderful figure of Christ. In the winter, how shapeless and unpromising is its appearance; cut down almost to the earth, leafless and branchless – "a root out of a dry ground," (Is 53. 2). Who could recognise that barren stump, in the luxiriant growth of autumn, clothed in abundant foliage, the green almost hidden by the wealth of purple grapes it bears. So Christ. Cut down at the Cross, He lives now in the power of resurrection life and fruitfulness. And His people, too, can be "filled with the fruits of righteousness which are by Jesus Christ," (Phil 1. 11). Who would have dared to foretell at that Cross, that a few weeks later, many of His very murderers would be kneeling at His feet, and that to-day, myriads, who never saw Him, would be willing by grace to die for His Name? But there are fruitless branches in this "True Vine" as well as fruitful. The Husbandman tends all. Those He *excises* by judgment, these He *exercises* by discipline. "Every branch in *Me* that beareth not fruit, He taketh away; and every branch that beareth fruit, He purgeth, that it may bring forth more fruit," (v 2). Note, the fruitless branch, is not a branch in the nominal Church – a mere professor in Christendom, not some foreign import nominally attached to the vine, but a branch in ME. This excision of a branch in the True Vine has been the subject of much controversy and questioning among believers. Can it be that one united to Christ, may be finally separated from Him, so as to be lost? To answer this satisfactorily, we must distinguish carefully between the various figures representing the relations of the Lord, to His people. Some of these imply eternal bonds of relationship; some only communion or privilege. There can be no separation where the eternal relationship and security of the believer is in view; there may be, where it is a question only of privilege, and service. Let us glance at some of these figures. In 1 Sam 25. 29, Abigail uses a beautiful figure to describe the relation of David to Jehovah. "The soul of my Lord shall be bound in the bundle of life with the Lord thy God." Here, the figure would seem to be that of a bundle of living stems, the true Israel bound up with the cords of love to Jehovah. It is a "bundle of life," and those cords are unbreakable. Then, in Jer 13, the Lord uses the figure of a girdle. The nation of Israel is the girdle, wherewith He has girded Himself. "As the girdle cleaveth to the loins of a man, so have I caused to cleave unto me *the whole house* of Israel, . . . that they might be unto Me for a People, and for a Name, and for a praise, and for a glory" (Jer 13. 11). Here the prophet tells us, the girdle is marred, and Israel, as a nation, is cut off from the place of privilege, though later, it is true, the remnant of the nation will be grafted in again to the olive (See also Rom 11).

Other Old Testament figures of the relation of the saints to their God, such as His "portion," His "inheritance," His "jewels," need not detain us. They all speak of the preciousness and inviolability of those who belong to Him. Certainly He would not allow His inheritance to be destroyed, or His "special treasure" (Mal 3. 17, marg.) to be lost.

There is, however, another figure, perhaps the most familiar of all, that of the flock of sheep, which claims attention. This is applied to Israel in the Old Testament, and also primarily to them in the New, as we see from such words of our Lord as "the lost sheep of the house of Israel" (Matt 15. 24), or in such as John 10. But in verse 16 of this chapter the figure is expanded to include "other sheep which are not of this fold," others of the redeemed outside the limits of Judah, who with them will form "one flock" under the "One Shepherd." In the former case, though they have "wandered far away o'er mountains cold," the promise of the Good Shepherd – Jehovah Himself – is, "I will seek out My sheep, and will deliver them out of all places, where they have been scattered in the cloudy and dark day" (Ezek 34. 12). But of the larger flock, He says, "My sheep hear My voice, and I know them, and they follow Me. And I give unto them eternal life, and they shall never perish, neither shall anyone pluck them out of My hand." And then, as though to remind them that those whom the Father gives into the Shepherd's hand, do not cease to be His (John 17. 9, 10), for He retains them in His own, He adds, "My Father that gave them Me, is greater than all, and no one is able to pluck them out of My Father's hand" (John 10. 28).

Next, there are the still stronger figures of the Bridegroom and bride, and of the Head and members. Clearly the Bridegroom cannot lose the bride, nor the Head one of His members. Here eternal security is writ large on both figures, for the loss of the bride would leave the Bridegroom bereft and solitary, and were the feeblest member severed from the body that body must for ever bear the blemish. But the Church will not only be holy, but "without blemish" (Eph 5. 27), so that not a single member will be lacking, in that day. This will not induce in the true believer, a spirit of carelessness, or of licence, but of absolute dependence on God, a holy fear, and the earnest cry, "Keep me!" "Hold Thou me up!" "Preserve my soul!"

But in the case before us, the figure is of a different order. A flock is numbered, and each sheep is known to the Shepherd and knows His voice. If one were missing, the flock would be incomplete. But whoever thought of counting the branches of a fruit tree? Not the most careful gardener; nor would he dream of naming all the sprouts, the buds, and tendrils of the vine. A few twigs more or less could make no difference. Moreover, excised branches can be grafted in again, as members of a body cannot. The Father, who preserves the sheep, cuts off the fruitless branch. But does this signify, as some would argue, that a child of God can perish? No, for we have seen this would be a flat contradiction of other Scriptures. Does it imply, on the other hand, that the excised branches were never *true* branches? Some indeed affirm so, and explain the position of the said branch as one of outward privilege, rather than of inward reality, as in the professing body of Christendom, rather than in the body of Christ. But though one must not press a figure too far, this branch must have sprouted out of the vine; it is the product of its life, and in this case, our Lord recognises even the "branch . . . that beareth not fruit" (v 2) as a true branch of the vine. He is not speaking of thorns or briars, for He calls this particular fruitless branch one of His own branches. "Every branch IN ME, that beareth not fruit, He taketh away" (v 2). It is "IN," really and vitally united; it is "in ME," not merely in the professing church, but "in Christ." Therefore, what we have here is, not God dealing with a lifeless professor, but the *Father* dealing with a failing child. It must be remembered that it is the "Father" who is the Husbandman. It may be doubted whether "the Father," as such, has anything to do with the world, or the world with Him. When we read of Him whom "The Father sent into the world," (John 10. 36) . . . the relationship emphasised is of that of the Sender with the Sent One, not of the Sender with the world. No doubt there are lifeless professors who have crept in unawares among the people of God, and it behoves us all not to take ourselves too easily for granted, especially if we are walking carelessly, but I submit it is not here a question of a false professor being cut off from his place of outward profession, and much less a child of God losing his place in the family, but of a *servant* of the Lord being *taken away* from his sphere of fruit-bearing. A child of God cannot be removed from the family, but a servant of Christ *may* be removed from his place of responsibility and usefulness, laid aside by physical infirmity, or even cut off by death. "Judgment must first begin at the house of God" (1 Pet 4. 17). We see this in the bright early days of the Church. The closer the unity of the people of God to one another and their communion with Him, the greater the energy of the Spirit in blessing, or in judgment.

Some may be surprised to hear the names of Ananias and Sapphira adduced in such a connection. No doubt their case was very serious, and their fall grievous. But there is no hint that they were habitual liars, nor is the question of their faith raised, in the passage. Is it unknown to-day for Christians to fall into lying? Were the possibility not contemplated the Holy Spirit would not utter such a warning as "Lie not one to another," (Col 3. 9). But falling into a sin, is not the same as *living* in sin. A clean beast may slip into the mire, an unclean one will wallow in it. If a professing Christian's course is characterised by sharp practice, unrighteousness, and lying, all his profession or preaching will not save him from the final judgment of God, except he repent. Ananias and Sapphira were cut off, not because their sin has been unique in the history of the Church, or is unparalleled even to-day, but because the Spirit's presence was then ungrieved, and therefore manifested in greater energy. A case of discipline, where the branch was only temporarily removed but was grafted in again, is that of the notorious sinner of 1 Cor 5. He was put away, that his spirit might be saved in "the day of the Lord Jesus," (v 5). Hymanæeus and Alexander (1 Tim 1. 20), apparently prominent and gifted men, were "delivered to Satan, that they might learn not to blaspheme". As to whether they ever learned their lesson and were proved real, we cannot say. The references to them, in the second Epistle, are ominous.

Perhaps a more directly apposite case would be that of the Corinthian saints in 1 Cor 11, who were chastened of the Lord, on account of their unworthy partaking of the Lord's Supper. "For this cause many are weak and sickly among you, and many sleep," (v 30). Here we see three degrees of discipline. Some became "weak", their strength for service suffered diminution; others became "sick," they were temporarily debarred from their opportunities of service; then lastly, some, in whom these dealings had no effect, "slept." the word specially used in the New Testament, for the death of believers. This last class were definitely cut off before their time from the possibility of earthly service. The reality of their faith is not questioned; indeed, it is implicitly affirmed, for they were chastened *"that they should not be condemned with the world,"* (1 Cor 10. 25).

The concluding portion of John 15 is taken up with the world's hatred to the disciples of the Lord. But He offers them a double consolation in verses 18-19. The same hatred had been manifested toward Him, its prior Object, and it also proved that they were "not of the world" (for like, loves like), but that He had "chosen them out of the world."The world would hate and persecute them for His Name's sake, through ignorance of Him, that sent Him. For, if they knew God – as they professed to do – how could they hate His sent One? But so perfectly did the Lord interpret the Father, that to hate Him whom they had seen, proved their hatred to Him whom they had not seen. "He that hateth Me, hateth My Father also" (ver 23).

Verses 22-24 call for special note. In what sense are we to understand the twice-repeated expression. "They had not had sin"? Is this to be taken in an *absolute* or *relative* sense? I think the word "cloak" (Gk. *pro-phasis* – excuse) points to the *latter* meaning. The contrast is not between sinlessness and sinfulness, but between being *with* or "without excuse." In verse 22, the presence of Christ and His *words* took away every excuse, which otherwise might have been alleged. In verse 24, had it not been for His *works,* of so unique a character, their responsibility would have been of a different order. As it was, it was aggravated by the fact of their having seen and hated both Christ and the Father. Added privilege, increases opportunity and responsibility.

> Light accepted, bringeth light;
> Light rejected, bringeth night.

In spite of this, the disciples would bear witness to Christ in the power of the Holy Spirit, whose mission it was to testify of Him. In chap 14. 16, the Spirit is the Father's gift, in answer to the Lord's prayer. Here it is the Lord, who promises to send Him from the Father, who "proceedeth from the Father" (v 26) shewing how far from the truth are they, who, in order ostensibly to establish the true humanity of Christ, present us with Him, as shorn of His Divine attributes. Were there any conflict between the two, either His humanity now, must be sacrificed or His Divine attributes, and that for ever.

The result of such teaching is, a confounding of the Divine and human natures of our Lord. Incarnation would not then be the Son of God, entering into Manhood, but His being, changed into man, ignorant and powerless, except so far as enlightened and empowered by the Father. All this, as is too sadly evident, is a deadly attack on the Person of Christ. For how can a Person be deprived of His proper attributes, and not be affected thereby? If this were the truth concerning Christ when down here, it is the truth concerning Him to-day on "the throne of God," for "He is the same yesterday, and *to-day,* and for ever," (Heb 13. 8) and we would have no Saviour who *knows us,* no High Priest to *help* us, and no *Lord, "in the midst."*

The true doctrine of God is, that personally the Lord was unchanged. He was at birth, "Wonderful, Counsellor, the Mighty God, the Everlasting Father, the Prince of Peace" (Isa 9. 6). But, in relation to the Father, He entered a sphere, till then unknown, that of Servant, and while retaining all His essential attributes, He placed them unreservedly and exclusively at the Father's disposal. In that sense, He never spake or acted "from Himself," (see John 14. 10) or on His own initiative. It was the Father who did the works. But on the other hand it was equally true that "What things so-ever the Father doeth, *these* also doeth the Son likewise" (John 5. 19).

How all this, shows the sinful folly of attempting to analyse and define the "great mystery of God – even Christ," or to explain the union of the Divine and human natures in the one Blessed Person, the Lord Jesus Christ. We do know, that the Eternal Word, who was God, *"became flesh"* (John 1. 14), that is, truly and completely man – apart from sin – and that those who saw His glory, saw the glory, as of "the only begotten of the Father," full of grace and truth. And that while He was down here, no less than *before* and *since,* "the whole fulness of God was pleased to dwell in Him" (Col 1. 11, RVm).

> All the Father's counsels claiming
> Equal glories for the Son;
> All the Son's effulgence beaming,
> Makes the Father's glory known.
>
> By the Spirit, all pervading.
> Hosts unnumbered round the Lamb,
> Crowd with light and joy unfading,
> Hail Him, as the great I am.

11

FORWARNING THEM (John 16)

THERE are certain things in this chapter, which the Lord – to spare His disciples – had not wished to tell them before (v 4), that is the persecutions that awaited them. "Hitherto" His presence had protected them; but *now* that He is leaving them, they must be forwarned. There were also "many things" (ver 12), that He had to say to them, which He could not tell them even then, for they were not able to bear them. For this, the Comforter first must come. But that could not be, until He Himself was glorified. So it was expedient that He sould go away (see v 7). In chap 14. 26, it is said to be the Father who would send the Spirit. Here, it is the Lord Himself. At Pentecost, both these promises were fulfilled.

Christ "having received of the Father the promise of the Holy Ghost, hath shed forth this, which ye now see and hear" (Acts 2. 33). Of course, the Lord had possessed the Spirit "without measure" in the days of His flesh, but not to communicate Him. Now, for the first time, He was to baptize His people (see John 1. 33) "in the Holy Spirit," into union with Himself, as members of His body. And this ministry of the Spirit would be twofold. First, toward the world, He would enforce on it the crowning sin of unbelief in Christ; His own "righteousness" – proved by His session on the Father's throne, and their "judgement," following in due course, that of its prince, (see vv 9-11). Secondly, the Spirit would guide His *disciples* into "all truth," (v 13) shewing them the things of Christ, and "things to come," (v 13) such being part of the many things, they were not yet able to bear from the lips of Christ then. Surely, this suffices to negative that unholy conception of a contrast between the teachings of Christ and of Paul. "Back to Jesus," is the cry of many to-day, who, as we have seen, have a vague idea, that the Lord's teaching was only ethical. They laud the Sermon on the Mount in order to evade the full teachings of the Epistles, as to the fall of man, redemption by blood, justification by faith, and coming judgment. But how shallow such a pretence is, is evident, when we consider as has been noted before, that there is not one outstanding truth revealed by the Spirit through Paul, James, Peter, John or Jude, which is not already found, at least in germ, in the Gospels. The same Spirit who spoke through our Lord, *wrote* through the apostles and prophets.

The Spirit was not to speak of Himself (*i.e.,* on His own initiative), but whatsoever He should hear, that He would speak. But no one pretends that the Holy Spirit laid aside His Divine attributes, and yet similar words to these (*e.g.* John 5. 19, 20; 8. 28), are quoted as proving this of our Lord, with what reason, may be judged. The whole assumption is radically false, and confounds the harmony and interdependence of Divine Persons, with what these men do not scruple to describe in referring to our blessed Lord, as His "ignorance" and "weakness."

But the departure of the Lord Jesus to the heavens has not interrupted, but intensified His interpretation of the Father. It was, as He revealed Himself down here, that the Father was revealed; now as He is revealed by the Spirit, in a deeper and wider measure, so is the Father correspondingly; and that not in parable, but in plain speech.

This would lead to more intimate fellowship with the Father. In that day, they would no longer ask[1] questions (*erotao*) of Him, they would make requests (*aiteo*) of the Father, and that for the first time *in His Name*. The prayer taught by the Lord to His disciples, was not in His Name, and was therefore temporary in character. But when they should make requests (*aiteo*) in His Name, the Lord did not promise to pray (*erotao*) the Father for them: that would be unnecessary, for the Father Himself loved them, because they had loved Him, and believed He came out from God. "We love Him because He first loved us" (1 John 4. 19), but it is no small thing to the Father, to find in this scene of carnal hate to Christ, some hearts loving Him. Such He

---

[1] "Erotao," translated "ask" in vv 5, 19, 23 (first ask), 30 and "pray" in v 26, also chap 17. 9, 15 and 20 means to enquire of or to pray to an equal. "Aiteo" is to "make request to a superior."

loves with a *special* love. The Lord closes with one more word of comfort. He had told them to expect tribulation. "In the world ye shall have tribulation" and He adds, "Be of good cheer; I have overcome the world" (v 33). This is true now and may be the realized experience of all the true children of God, while *in* the world.

12

INTERCEDING FOR THEM (John 17)

THOUGH our Lord was pre-eminent in His prayer-life, as in all else, we could form but a meagre conception of the character of His prayers, had it not pleased God to leave on record this wonderful example of intercession, contained in John 17. It is as though our Lord wished us to know how He prays for us *now*. This chapter has been called "Our Lord's Priestly Prayer." If so, it was by anticipation and of a new order, even the heavenly. "For if He were on earth, He would not be a priest," not being of the priestly tribe. Now, in ascension glory He is "a priest for ever, after the order of Melchizedek," (Heb 5. 6) and thus He "ever liveth to make intercession" (Heb 7. 25) for us.

In John, chapter 13 we have seen the Lord cleansing, as at the laver, His disciples' feet, as did the priests of old before entering the tabernacle (Exod 30. 17). In the chapters that follow, we may see something corresponding to the furniture of the holy place, the ministry of Christ illuminating His disciples by His Word, the candlestick; shewing them Himself as the object of their faith and spiritual sustenance, the table of shewbread; and becoming, in the revelation of His person, like a sweet incense ascending to the Father, the golden altar. Now, He leads them into the Holiest of all in the Heavenly Temple, the House of God, not made with hands, and so initiates them into the secrets of His communion with the Father. It might be profitably studied in this aspect among others. But it is rather as a declaration of the Father's Name, that I propose now to consider it.

He is declared here:

1. "As the Great **GIVER,** not only of "every good gift and every perfect gift" (James 1. 17) to us, but also as the Fountain of the Trinity: that is, the Source and Originator of all Divine counsels and blessings. For, though all the Three Persons are co-equal, co-eternal, and co-substantial, they do not all exercise the same functions in the Godhead. The first gift is "*glory.*" If the Son is to be glorified, it must be by the Father; "Father . . . glorify Thy Son, that Thy Son also may glory Thee," (v 1) not with a new glory, but "with the glory which I had with Thee before the world was;" nor must it be apart from the Father; "with Thine own self" (v 5).

In verse 22, He speaks of this glory as already bestowed, and at His disposition to bestow on His own. Truly, His words at the grave of Lazarus might be written across this whole prayer, I know "that Thou hearest Me always." (John 11. 42) In Mark 11. 24, the Lord exhorts us to believe "we have received," as soon as we ask, and here does so Himself. In verse 22, the glory seems to be connected with the gift of the Holy Ghost, by whom the unity of the body of Christ is formed and secured, "that they may be one, even as We are one."

The *recipients* of eternal life are another gift of the Father to Christ, for they are described all through the chapter as "them whom Thou has given Me," (see eg v 6). "Thine they were, and Thou gavest them Me; and they have kept Thy Word" (v 6), and they are still the Father's. "All Mine are

Thine and Thine are Mine; and I am glorified in them" (v 10).

The third gift is *power* (lit, authority) "over all flesh," (v 2) an authority exercised in the case of His own in giving them eternal life. The original is hard to render, but the RV is far nearer it than the AV, "that whatsoever Thou hast given Him" (lit, every thing, *i.e.*, the company of the redeemed viewed as a whole), to them He should give eternal life, for they must receive it as individuals.

Then fourthly, the very *work* He had finished, was a gift of the Father, "I have finished the work Thou gavest Me to do," (v 4). The Lord did not merely "do *something* for God," but the work the Father gave Him to do, so we too are "created in Christ Jesus unto good works, which God hath before prepared, that we should walk in them," (Eph 2. 10 m). Nor did He speak His own words, but the Word of God in the very words of God, "I have given unto them the words which Thou gavest Me" (v 8). These words then were yet another gift to Christ.

2. The second character in which the Father is revealed in this prayer, is as the **KEEPER** of Christ's people; "Holy Father, keep them in Thy Name, which Thou hast given Me" (v 11, RV). The Lord, while with them, had kept them in the Father's Name, and none of them was lost, but (in contrast with such) the Son of Perdition was lost. Compare for a similar construction, Luke 4. 26, 27, where the widow of Sarepta and Naaman are clearly not exceptions to, but in contrast with, what has gone before.

Connected with this assurance of being in the hands of the Father, come our Lord's words, "These things I speak in the world, that they might have My joy fulfilled in themselves," (v 13). And no wonder, for what better ground of rejoicing can we have than to know for surety, that we are in the hands of an infinitely tender Father, full of solicitude for our highest good, to whom we belong by election, creation, redemption and adoption? He it was who gave us to the Son, who has handed us back to the Father to keep for Him.

As to the manner of this keeping, it is revealed in the next character of the Father, here displayed:-

3. THE **SANCTIFIER,** and the safeguards are not legal but moral, not of peculiar dress, but inwardly of the heart; not of material walls, but of spiritual principles. Believers are not to be taken out of the world like hermits, but preserved like "strangers and pilgrims" in it; "Sanctify them through Thy truth: Thy word is truth," (v 17). And it was in order that the word might be able to exercise its separating effect, that the Lord separated Himself by death and resurrection, for it was only thus the Spirit could come, and render the word effective.

And all this He prays, not only for the eleven, but for believers in Him, by their testimony up to the end, that they, too, may form part of the one body. This unity is spiritual and Divine, and will only be openly manifested when the Lord returns for His own, from every clime and nation. Then, I would submit, the world will believe, when they see the vacant places everywhere, but not on Christ as Saviour, but merely in His Divine mission, "that Thou hast sent Me" (v 23), which is not necessarily saving faith at all. Later, the world will not only believe, but *know* this, when Christ returns in glory *with* all His saints, because the oneness of the body will then be manifested complete and perfect. That christians ought to keep the unity of the Spirit is true, but have grievously failed is too sadly evident. But I do not judge that this is what the Lord is asking for here, otherwise, as all His prayers must be answered, the outward unity of believers would have been perfectly preserved down the ages; but rather that their integral unity should be assured to the end, by their baptism in the Spirit, into one body.

We are not exhorted to keep the unity of the body, which

is guaranteed, not by the well meant efforts of christians of different denominations to unite from time to time for prayer and gospel effort – at best an imperfect and partial thing, but by this prayer of Christ; the promise of the Father, and the indwelling of the Holy Spirit. But we are told to "keep the unity of the Spirit in the bond of peace," "with all lowliness and meekness, with long-suffering, forbearing one another in love," and that on the basis of the sevenfold unity detailed in the following verses (Eph 4. 4-6).

4. The last Revelation of the Father in this prayer is as the **LOVER** of His people. The world is to know that the love of the Father to His people is commensurate with His love to Christ, a love which was in exercise before the foundation of the world. Not only does the Lord desire that His people should be with Him, to behold His glory, but that the love wherewith the Father loves Him should be in them and He in them, as a present enjoyed reality, and each be able to say with confidence –

> The love wherewith He loves the Son,
> Such is His love to me.

It is with this end in view that our Lord declares the Father's Name, and this prayer was the culmination not of His interpretation of the Father, but of it, while in this scene, for it was not complete, for He adds, "and will declare it," (v 26). The testimony was continued by Him in the Epistles and the Revelation, through the Spirit, and will continue for ever in Heaven.

THE UNCHANGING LOVE.

He loved me 'ere Creation dawn
   Had decked the mountain and hill;
Befor the evening and the morn,
   He loved me and He loves me still.

He loved me 'ere the stream of years
   Had pierced its source, a tiny rill;
(How soon to swell a surge of tears!)
   He loved me and He loves me still.

He loved me when my deadly sin
   Did bitter wrath for Him distil;
When losing all my soul to win,
   He loved me and He loves me still.

He loved me when, a captive led,
   My will embraced His sovereign will,
And kissed the piercèd hand that bled;
   He loved me and He loves me still.

Then when enthralled by grace divine,
   I prayed Him heart and soul to fill,
That I might for His glory shine,
   He loved me and He loves me still.

And when with Him beyond the skies,
   Though raptures new my spirit thrill,
This well-known song shall ever rise –
   He loved me and He loves me still.

WH

The Christ
of
God

HIS PRE-EMINENCE – HIS SELF-ABASEMENT.

LUTHER once compared the Old and New Testaments to the spies, who bore back between them, on a staff, the grapes of Eschol (Num 13. 23). Of these two men, though they both shared the same burden, the hindermost alone could gaze upon the spoil. So Christ is the burden of all Scripture; but while the Old Testament truly "spake of Him", it is in the New, pre-eminently, that we "behold His glory." The object now is to present for our contemplation and meditation some of the glories and excellences of the Person of Christ, as displayed to us in Col 1. 15-19 and Phil 2. 5-16 – two rich bunches from the great "cluster" of "The Word."

We will consider these two important passages under the descriptive titles of "The Pre-eminence of Christ" and "The Self-abasement of Christ."

THE CHRIST OF GOD:

1

THE PRE-EMINENCE OF CHRIST

COLOSSIANS 1. 15-19

"Who is the image of the invisible God the first-born of every creature: for by Him were all things created . . . and for Him: and He is before all things, and by Him all things consist, and He is the Head of the body, the Church: who is the beginning, the first-born from the dead; that in all things He might have the pre-eminence. For it pleased the Father that in Him should all fulness dwell."

WE have before us in this passage one of the familiar fields of Scripture. Familiarity, even with Scripture, though much to be desired, may have its dangers. Let us not then be as men who merely traverse a field by some well-beaten track, but rather like those who cultivate the soil – or better still, like miners who dig beneath the surface for hid treasure.

We have in this passage a singularly full presentation of the Person of our Lord Jesus Christ. It is good ever to have before us the greatness and glories of His Person. First, because the adequacy and value of a work depend on the competency and worth of the worker. These verses give us a portrait of a great and wondrous Person framed in crimson – the crimson of His blood. This blood is said in verse 14 to bring us redemption – the forgiveness of sins, and in verse 20, to be the ground of our peace and of our reconciliation with God. The important question then arises, Whose blood is it? The passage we are about to consider assures us that the One who shed it is "Mighty to save". But the assurance of this fact not only gives rest to the conscience, it presents a worthy object to the heart. The Colossians were turning aside "to philosophy and vain deceit," as, alas! so many are doing in our day. How did the apostle meet the need? By presenting to them the Person of Christ to attract and satisfy their hearts. There is also a third reason why the Spirit of God delights in exalting the Person of the Lord, and it is the most important of all reasons, that He may be glorified, and that God may be glorified in Him.

The Satanic promise to man in Eden was, "Ye shall be as gods," and to-day we hear voices of "sinister resemblance," which seem to say that the time cannot be far distant, when Satan's man shall arise, "who shall exalt himself above all that is called God." But the Divine purpose concerning Christ is "That in all things *He* might have the pre-eminence," (v 18) and that purpose shall stand.

I believe we have in this passage a **ninefold testimony** to the pre-eminence of that Blessed Person, whom we know as the Lord Jesus Christ. Some persons seem hardly happy, unless they can find the number seven in Scripture; but there are other numbers besides seven, important as that number is. Why, for instance, is the fruit of the Spirit ninefold? Why have we nine characteristics of the blessed man in Matt 5, and only nine recorded appearances of our risen Lord? I think the key may be found in I Cor 12. 7-10, where we have a ninefold "manifestation of the Spirit given to every man to profit withal." The number nine would thus seem to stand for perfection or fulness of manifestation. So here, we have a ninefold or perfect manifestation of the pre-eminence of Christ, dividing itself into three groups of three divisions each, of which the first group looks back to a past eternity, the second to our Lord's earthly ministry, and the third to His resurrection glories.

We have then:

1. A testimony to our Lord's pre-eminence as the ONLY BEGOTTEN SON. (a) As *Creator* (v 16), (b) as *"before all things"* (v 17), (c) as the *Preserver* of all (v 17).

2. A testimony to His pre-eminence as the INCARNATE ONE. (a) As the *Image* of God (v 15), (b) as *the First-born of every creature* (v 15), (c), as the Reservoir of all *fulness* (v 19).

3. A testimony to His pre-eminence as the RISEN ONE. (a) As the *First-born from the dead* (v 18), (b), as the *Head of the Church* (v 18), (c) as *the Heir of all things* (v 16).

1. Let us then first consider Him as the **ONLY BEGOTTEN SON OF GOD.** (a) As *Creator*. Verse 16 tells us, "By Him were all things created that are in heaven and that are in earth, visible and invisible," including the highest spiritual intelligences of the universe –Cherubim, Seraphim, the Archangel, yea, Satan himself, as well as material worlds and systems. "Without Him was not anything made that was made." This takes us back to the "beginning" of Gen 1.1 It is true we have the Triune Elohim mentioned as Creator in this verse, and yet we know from other Scriptures that it was the Son who was the Executive of the Trinity in creation, as we read in Heb 1. 2, "By whom also He made the worlds." In Proverbs 8. 30 (RV), there is a remarkable change from the AV, which bears out what has been said. Wisdom is speaking. "When He prepared the heavens, I was there . . . when He gave the sea His decree . . . then I was with Him (not, as one brought up with Him, but) as a Master Workman." And Zech 12. tells us that the One, who was pierced by Israel, to their present loss and future sorrow (v 10) was the very one who, in verse 1, is said to have "stretched forth the heavens, laid the foundation of the earth, and formed the spirit of man within him." Had there never been redemption to accomplish He could still have rightly claimed the homage of the universe as Creator. Thus it is noteworthy that in Rev 4. 11, glory and honour are ascribed to the One who

"created all things," before He is worshipped as the Lamb in the following chapter, on the ground of accomplished redemption.

(b) The second claim of our Lord to pre-eminence as the **ONLY BEGOTTEN SON OF GOD** is based on the fact of His *pre-existence.* "He is before all things" (v 17). He is the Eternal One. This takes us back further than "the beginning" of Gen 1. 1, to that shoreless eternity of John 1. 1, "In the beginning was the Word, and the Word was with God, and the Word was God." If, as we have seen, Wisdom could say in Prov 8., "When He prepared the heavens, I was there," He could also say, "The Lord possessed Me in the beginning of His way, *before His works of old.*" He is thus independent of and outside of Creation, in contradiction to that bastard Pantheism of to-day, with its vain talk about the "Immanence of God," which seeks to confound Creator and Creation, and would really rob us of a Personal God.

This fundamental truth of the pre-existence of the Son is borne witness to with signal clearness in many Scriptures, and notably in the Gospel of John. The Forerunner, taught of God, could say of Him who, according to the flesh, was his younger cousin, "He is preferred before me, for *He was before me*" (John 1. 30). The Lord could speak (and who else could possibly have done so?) of ascending to that place *where He was before* (chap 6. 62), and could testify to His enemies, *"Before Abraham was, I AM"* (chap 8. 58). And when in His sacerdotal prayer He asked to be glorified as Son of Man, He could ask no greater glory than that which He had had with the Father as Son of God *"before the world was."* In Col 1. the Spirit of God takes us back further still, and testifies saying, "He is before all things."

(c) The third point of our Lord's pre-eminence as the **ONLY BEGOTTEN SON OF GOD,** consists in His being the *Sustainer of all things.* "By Him all things (not only exist but) consist" (v 17), that is, hold together, or as we have read in Heb 1. 3, "He is upholding all things by the Word of His power." Men, if they dare not deny God altogether, would gladly put Him as far away, or as far back as possible. But we believe in creation, not in evolution; in a sustaining God, not in blind laws working automatically and independently of the present will of the Creator. A man was asked one day what kind of a Christian he was. He replied, "I belong to the *Dependents*." "I suppose you mean the Independents," said the other. "No, I am just dependent on God all the time." And so is this universe, and so are we all, though we may not as intelligently or as practically recognise it as this Christian did. Yet this is our true relation toward God, and He would have us take it more simply.

> "Worlds on worlds are hanging on His hand;
> Life and death are waiting His command:
> Yet His tender bosom makes thee room."

"Blessed is the man that trusteth in Him." (Psa 34. 8). May we each be able to say with a well-known saint, now with Christ, "I am that blessed man!" We have thus seen the pre-eminence of our Lord, as having created all things, as having preceded all things, and as preserving all things.

We now come to the second great phase of manifestation, in which we view our Lord in **INCARNATION.**

(a) He is pre-eminent in Incarnation because "He is the image of the invisible God" (v 15). We must distinguish carefully between the appearances of Jehovah in the Old Testament and the unique and unalterable condition assumed by our Lord in Incarnation. We must also distinguish between the sense in which Adam was made "in the image of God," and that in which the Lord Jesus WAS "the image of the invisible God." Never in his state of innocence could Adam have said with propriety, as our Lord did, "He that beholdeth Me, beholdeth Him that sent Me" (John 12. 45,); "He that hath seen Me hath seen the Father" (John 14. 9). When Eve saw Adam before the fall, she saw one in moral semblance to God, and capable of enjoying communion with his Maker, and of growing in likeness to Him – but only a man. But Jesus was the "image of the Invisible God." Now an image is not a shadow. The two things are distinguished in Heb. 10. 1: "The law having a *shadow* of good things to come, and not the very *image*." Its sacrifices, its sanctuary, and its priesthood were but shadows. The Romish priesthood, which is an attempt at a literal reproduction of certain features of the Jewish pattern, is a mere counterfeit of a shadow, and the Anglican priest is a mere copy of a counterfeit. And what are we to day of the "minister," who, while professing to teach the priesthood of all believers, really usurps their priesthood, save this, that he, without suspecting it, commits an act which, under the law, was punishable with death (Num 3. 10; 4. 15). Now a shadow differs from an image in that it bears witness to an objective reality, whereas an image, in Scriptural language is, I believe, the thing itself MADE VISIBLE. Thus vapour might be said, in a sense, to be the image of steam. It is the invisible made visible. God forbade Israel to make "any image" of Himself, for what could any man-made image of the Invisible God be but a miserable caricature? What were the idols of the nations? Mere blind, dumb, deaf, helpless blocks, though they had eyes, mouths, ears, hands, and feet (Psa 115. 4-7). On the other hand the Spirit of God represents Jehovah as seeing, hearing, speaking, handling, though He had no corresponding members or similitude (Exod 3. 7, 8). In the Lord Jesus Christ we have not a shadow of God, but "the very *image*." In His looks of compassion, in His ever-open ear, in His hands stretched forth to bless, in His feet ever bent on errands of mercy, and above all, in that blessed form nailed to the Cross of Calvary, we see the heart of God toward needy, sinful man. It is the purpose of God, for which all things work together, that the people of God should be conformed to the image of Christ; but to Him will ever belong the pre-eminence of having been down here, in all His ways and words and works – "the image of the Invisible God."

(b) In Incarnation too He was "the *First-born* of every creature" (v. 15). This expression has been explained to mean, that He was the First-born; *before* every creature; but I submit that this will not hold true because as the Eternal One He was the only-begotten, not the first-born son. Coming as the expression does directly after the one we have just considered, I think it is plain we must connect it with His presence on this earth as the Incarnate One. Not that He became, as is now said, the First-born of humanity, in the sense of taking humanity into union with Himself by incarnation. Every truly spiritual mind must instinctively recoil from such deadly error. Even as far as His people were concerned, had He not died and risen again, He must ever have continued to abide "alone." I Chron 5. 1 may throw light on this subject, by way of illustration. Reuben, Israel's first-born, lost his birthright through his sin, but it did not descend to Simeon or Levi, or even to Judah, from whom sprang the royal family of Israel. It remained in abeyance for many years, until it was eventually bestowed on Ephraim and Manasseh (Gen 48. 5). Adam, too, lost his birthright through his transgression, and no one was found who could claim the first-born's place, till He came "whose right it was" Jesus took the first-born's place, not only because He was the best and holiest, but because of what He was in Himself, for what other place could the Creator have in becoming flesh and tabernacling among His creatures, than the first place? And this the "for" connecting verses 15 and 16 shows.

(c) The third point on which rests the pre-eminence of our Lord (and let us not forget that all these claims are cumulative) is that *"in Him all the fulness was pleased to dwell"* (v 19). We hear much to-day of an "emptied" Christ – self-emptied, if you will, but emptied for all that. But what we need is a full Christ, not an empty Christ, and it was just such an One that God was pleased to give us. In my judgement the AV of Phil 2. 7, "He made Himself of no reputation," agrees with the context better than the Revised, "He emptied Himself"; for it was not of all that He was as God that He consented to be deprived, but of that particular mode of existence which was proper and peculiar to Him as only equal with God. I would suggest that "He effaced Himself"[1] better conveys the thought of the passage than "He emptied Himself." He ever and always was a Divine Person. In Him dwelt all the fulness of the Deity bodily, but He held it in abeyance, in subservience to His Father as the perfect Servant. It is true that only in resurrection could this fulness be communicated to His own. But it was in Him down here. To this the Apostle John bears witness when he says, "We beheld His glory, the glory of the only begotten of the Father, full of grace and truth" (John 1. 14). His moral glory was only visible to anointed eyes, but to such it was seen in fulness.

Now we come to the third cord, with its three-fold manifestation of our Lord's pre-eminence in **RESURRECTION.**

(a) "He is the *beginning – the First-born from the dead.*" I think this expression "beginning" should be connected with that title of our Lord in Rev 3. 14, "The beginning of the creation of God" – that is, of course, of the New Creation. This became true of Him in resurrection, and is therefore closely linked with the expression which follows in our passage, "the First-born from the dead." As the only begotten Son of God, there always was, and always must be, an infinite distance between Him and the highest of His creatures. As the First-born of every creature, we have seen, He must have ever remained "alone," had He not "fallen

---

[1] The rendering proposed by Dr Lightfoot, "He stripped Himself", would seem to favour this suggestion.

into the ground and died"; but as the First-born from the dead, He is "the First-fruits," the beginning of the New Creation. As such, He has entered a sphere where death can no longer have dominion over Him. He was the first to snap the chains of death, and to come forth Victor from the grave, and in so doing He becomes "the First-born of many brethren," all destined to be conformed to His image and to share His glory.

(b) Secondly, *"He is the Head of the Church."* "He loved the Church and gave Himself for it, that He might sanctify and cleanse it . . . and present it to Himself a glorious Church" (Eph 5. 24-29). Therefore it is to Him that the Church is subject, it is on Him that the Church depends. If religious men make so much of those whom they have themselves appointed heads of their great worldly systems, how much more should we of Him whom God has raised up and seated at His own right hand, and given to be Head over all things to the Church, which is His body. He is, as we have seen, "the First-born from the dead," and His Church is called "the Church of the first-born ones" (Heb 12. 23). Much has been said about meeting on "the ground of the one body." I think what is more Scriptural and more important is to meet in subjection to the one Head. He must be the centre of every true unity. The only way to keep the "unity of the Spirit" is to "hold the Head" – not merely the truth of it, important as that is – but the Head Himself as the Source of all supply and authority in the Church, which is His body, the Lord Jesus Christ.

(c) Lastly, the Lord is pre-eminent as the *"Heir of all things."* All things were "created by Him and for Him." He is the God-appointed Saviour, "whom God hath set forth to be a propitiation through faith in His blood" (Rom 3. 25). He is the God-appointed "High Priest," for "Christ glorified not Himself to be made High Priest" (Heb 5. 5) but God said unto Him, "Thou art My Son, this day have I begotten Thee" (Heb 5. 5). He is the divinely-apppointed Heir – for

Him hath God appointed Heir of all things (Heb 1. 3). Satan and Adam, in positions of responsibility, failed; but the stability of the universe is henceforth assured. For the "Heir of all things" is the Man of Calvary – the Divine Creator and Sustainer of all things.

2

THE SELF-ABASEMENT OF CHRIST (PHIL 2. 5-6)

IN the previous chapter we have passed in review some of the glories of the Son of God, "from everlasting to everlasting." (Psa 90. 2). It is true that we have viewed Him in the course of our survey in His path down here as the "Word become flesh." (John 1. 14). But even thus He has been presented to us not so much in His humiliation and suffering as in the intrinsic dignity and competency of His wondrous Person; not so much as He appeared to the world around, but as He appeared to the eye of faith and as He was in the mind of God, the One of whom John said, "We beheld His glory, the glory as of the only begotten of the Father, full of grace and truth." (John 1. 14). The passage we are about to consider (almost in contrast with the previous one) is concerned chiefly with what He became for the fulfilment of the Divine purposes, in humiliation and obedience unto death. What is more: the very height of glory to which we see Him exalted is in proportion to and commensurate with the depth of abasement to which He descended. We might compare the manifestation of Him in the Colossian passage to the Shhekinah glory in the tabernacle in the wilderness, but here to the manna outside on the sand of the wilderness itself. In this profound passage there are doubtless "some things hard to be understood," but the truths it contains are peculiarly necessary in the present day. Let us count upon the Spirit's teaching, and hold fast what is revealed.

The occasion of this deeply important passage was incipient failure among the saints at Philippi. We owe many precious portions of the Word of God to a similar cause. Take, for example, the Epistle to the Corinthians. Should we, humanly speaking, have had the eleventh chapter but for their disorders, the thirteenth but for their dissensions, or the fifteenth but for the denials by some among them of the Resurrection? This does not, of course, minimise the sin of failure, but rather magnifies the grace and wisdom of the Lord, in causing even the failures of His people to work together for the eventual blessing of the whole Church.

The condition of the Philippian saints was, on the whole, such as to bring joy to the apostle. The "ifs" of the first verse — "*If* there be therefore any consolation in Christ, *if* any comfort of love" — do not imply the contrary. The apostle *had* experienced consolation among them, but there was a "little cloud like a man's hand," among them, the appearing of which troubled him. They were not all of one mind (*e.g.*, chap 4. 2). Hence the exhortation, "Fulfil ye my joy that ye be like-minded" (*Gk.,* "that ye mind the same thing"). In the third chapter, where it is a question of blessed, though imperfect, Christian attainment, the apostle cites his own example, "Be ye followers together of me." (3. 17). Here, where he would present to them the perfect Christian standard, he can only point to the Perfect One. "Let this mind be in you which was also in Christ Jesus" (v 5). "Only by pride cometh contention" (Prov 13. 10). To live in harmony, we must be minded as He was minded. Thus Christ is presented in His person and work as the true corrective for their failure. Those who have fallen victims to "The New Apostacy" have done so because their condition was analogous to that described in the Gospel as "empty, swept, and garnished" (Matt 12. 44) – empty of the truth, prepared for "the lie." Our only preservative is to have Christ dwelling in our "hearts by faith" (Eph 3. 17), and His Word "dwelling in us richly" (Col 3. 16). We need not even study the blasphemous conceits of the day, we should rather avoid them. Like the pilot who claimed no profound acquaintance with the rocks and reefs, but only with the navigable channel, we need only know the truth of God to avoid the errors of the times. To use our Lord's own simile: Those who know the shepherd's voice will flee from the voice of strangers (John 10. 5). The voice of the Good Shepherd is connected in the minds of the sheep with *feeding*; that of the strange shepherd with *fleecing*. The one attracts, the other repels.

We have here the Lord presented to us in His Person and Work in three aspects.

1. As regards **His Eternal Condition:** "Being in the form of God."

2. As regards **His Determinate Counsel:** "He thought it not robbery to be equal with God."

3. As regards **the carrying out of this determinate counsel,** which involved **(A) a threefold** *action* **on His part** – (a) His *Renunciation.* "He made Himself of no reputation, and took upon Him the form of a servant." (b) His *Incarnation.* "He was made in the likeness of men." (c) His *Humiliation.* "Being found in fashion as a man He humbled Himself, and became obedient unto death, even the death of the cross." **(B) A threefold** *result* **on God's part** – (a) His *Exaltation:* "Wherefore God also hath highly exalted Him." (b) His *Designation* as Lord, "and hath given Him a Name which is above every name." (c) His *Recognition* and *Acclamation* by heavenly, earthly, and infernal beings. **(C) A threefold** *responsibility* **on our part** – (a) As to *Life:* "Work out your own salvation with fear and trembling." (b) As to *Walk:* "Do all things without murmurings and disputings." (c) As to *Testimony;* "Holding forth the Word of Life."

1. Let us first consider **THE ETERNAL CONDITION** of our Lord, as described in the words, "Being in the form of God." In this one pregnant sentence, the Spirit marks the greatness of the Person of Christ, and the height of glory from which He stooped. It is important to seize the exact meaning of the word "form" [Gr., *morphe*] in this and the following verse. The word has various meanings in English. It often means simply "shape" – *e.g.*, Ezek 10. 8: "There appeared in the cherubims the *form* of a man's hand under the wings." But when we say that a substance exists in a certain form, we do not necessarily refer to its shape at all, but we mean that this is the usual condition in which it is found, or, in other words, its ordinary "mode" of existence. It is this latter sense that the word is used in both places in this passage. "Being in the form of God" does not mean that our Lord before His incarnation was in the shape of God, for God is spirit, and has neither shape nor similitude. Nor does it imply, as some erroneously teach, that He had then any visible form, but that His eternal mode of existence was that of God, and in that from eternity He had subsisted (for that is the meaning of the strong word translated "being"), *only* as the Son of God, of the same substance as the Father, nothing lower, nothing else than a Divine Person. As Bengel has well said, "He who was in the form of God, could only be God." How far we are, and must ever be from fully apprehending what is involved in "being God" – eternal self-existence and self-sufficiency, inexhaustible resources of wisdom, knowledge, and power – infinite perfection of glories and excellencies, and how much more beside! And yet it was the One who "was God" (John 1, 1), who "became flesh and dwelt among us" (John 1. 14). Let us remember that if He who was and is in "the form of God" (though not now exclusively so) "became in the likeness of man," we are and ever will be only in the form of man. Though all believers do become "partakers of the divine nature" (2 Pet 1. 4), having been begotten of His

own will by the word of truth, there will always be an infinite disparity between the Deity and the highest of His creatures: their glorious privilege ever being to worship Him, His rightful due to receive their worship.

2. Now follow the words which tell of our Lord's **DETERMINATE COUNSEL.** They are so poorly rendered in the AV – "thought it not robbery to be equal with God." This sentence is ambiguous as it stands. It might mean that our Lord, before His incarnation, refrained from grasping at something He did not possess, namely, equality with God. But we have just seen that He was "in the form of God," therefore equal with God, so that this interpretation cannot stand. Others, again, interpret the phrase to mean that our Lord did not consider it robbery to be what He really was, namely, equal with God; but this makes of the phrase a merely confirmatory statement of the truth of the words "being in the form of God," The word "but" in the following verse shows that the sentence we are considering is not confirmatory of what precedes, but preparatory to what follows. Alford's translation bears this out, and gives, I believe, the true sense. "He deemed not His equality with God a matter for grasping," or, in other words, a thing to be held tenaciously. The leading thought of the word translated "a matter for grasping" (*harpagmon*) is not "snatching *from* another," but "snatching *for* oneself." (See Alford's New Testament on Philippians.) The words before us then mean that our Lord determined not to insist on being, as had always been His undisputed right, *only* in equality with God. When did this become His determinate counsel? We are not told. We might answer the question did we know when the Book referred to in Psalm 40. 7, 8 was written: "Lo I come, in the volume of the Book it is written of Me, I delight to do Thy will, O my God." Doubtless it was one of the eternal counsels of God that this should be. The Lord, on His part, would not stand on His Divine dignity

and rights, though He had such in infinite measure. We have no rights to speak of, and the man who stands on his dignity has very little standing ground. But are there many who willingly forego their rights, and leave their dignity in the hands of Him "who judgeth righteously"?

3

RENUNCIATION, INCARNATION AND HUMILIATION (PHIL 2.7-8)

THE determinate counsel of our Lord, to which we have referred, involved three things for Him.

(a) **RENUNCIATION.** He "made Himself of no reputation, and took upon Him the form of a servant." (v 7). The rendering of the AV suits, in my judgment, as I have said above, the context and facts better than that of the RV does. The change was rather one of relation than of prerogative. He was ever a Divine person, but He renounced His right of being ONLY in the form of God, by taking upon Him the "form of a servant." This does not mean that in taking the latter He ceased to be in the former. He did not empty Himself of His Divine prerogatives. These were part of Himself. It is true He veiled the glory which He had with the Father before the world was, and He was full of moral glory. Blind teachers, with their baseless *theories* of the "Kenosis,"[1] would make Him "altogether such an one as themselves," or even lower. But of which of them could it be said, "Now are we sure that Thou knowest all things" (John 16. 30), or which of

---

[1] Substantive from the Greek verb, literally translated, "He emptied himself."

them possesses the Divine prerogative, not only of "knowing all men," but of even knowing what is "in man" (John 2. 24, 25; Jer 17. 10). He had the Divine consciousness of His own inerrancy and infallibility. What more characterises the true people of God in every age, than a humble sense of imperfection or unworthiness, or waht was more inculcated by the teaching of our Lord? Yet He Himself never recalls a word, regrets an action, nor acknowledges a failure. Such phrases as "I wish I had, or had not," "Had I known, I would not," are entirely absent from His utterances. Then again, as has been well remarked, a whole group of phrases, common in the everyday speech of all peoples, must be sought for in vain in the records of our Lord's sayings – such expressions as "I think," "I believe," "I suppose," "I hope." On the contrary, His speech was ever characterised by certainty, and to His enemies He could say, "Which of you convinceth Me of sin?" (John 8. 46). Speaking of His relation to His Father He says, "I do always those things that please Him." (John 8. 29). Nevertheless, so complete was His self-effacement that, though He was "the Power of God," He could "do nothing of Himself" (John 5. 19); though He was "the Wisdom of God," His doctrine was not His own, but His that sent Him (John 7. 16); though He was the "Word become flesh," He would only speak the Father's words. He entirely disclaimed all initiative and originality, and was content ever to be the servant of the Father. Again, let it be noted that the expression, "took upon Him the form of a servant," does not mean that He became a servant in appearance only, but in addition to being in the form of God He really and truly became the dependent and obedient bond-slave. Though "knowing all things," He could say, "As I hear, I judge" (John 5. 30); "My doctrine is not Mine, but His that sent Me" (John 7. 16); and "Even as the Father said unto Me, so I speak" (John 12. 50). Though competent for all things, He thus spake of Himself: "The

Son can do nothing of Himself, but what he seeth the Father do" (John 5. 19); "The Father that dwelleth in Me, He doeth the works" (John 14. 10); "As the Father gave Me commandment, even so I do" (John 14. 31). Though His will was perfect, He could truly say, "I do not My own will" (John 5. 30; 6. 38). He would not use His power to make stones bread, though, as the Son of God, He could have of those same stones raised up chidlren to Abraham. He had the right to claim the throne, but He did not even claim a place to lay His head. Other servants God has had, but self and sin has always marred, in a measure, their brightest service. Here all was perfection and on Him Jehovah would fix all eyes with the words, "Behold My servant, whom I have chosen," (Isa 43. 10) as though there were none else than He. It is very interesting to notice the difference between the word translated bond-slave – *doulos* – and that often rendered minister – *diakonos*. Both words occur in the first verse of our Epistle. Paul entitles himself and Timothy "the bond-slaves of Jesus Christ," and he addresses among others the "deacons" or ministering brethren in the church at Philippi. A deacon (from a word meaning "to pursue"[2]) is a man viewed in relation to some particular service to which he is called and for which he is fitted. Paul, for instance, calls himself and Apollos "deacons" (Greek) by whom the Corinthians had believed (1 Cor 3. 5). In Romans 15. 8 the Lord Jesus is spoken of as "the deacon [Greek] of the circumcision to confirm the promises made unto the fathers," and Timothy who, as an apostolic delegate, and doubtless a "bishop" or overseer (though erroneously styled in a footnote to some of our Bibles *the first bishop* of the Ephesians, or else what becomes of the *bishops* of Acts 20. 28, RV?), is told by Paul that if he "put the brethren in remembrance of these things he will be a good *deacon* [Greek] of Jesus Christ" (I Tim 4. 6). I only quote these

---

[2] See R C Trench on the "Synonyms of the New Testament." Baker Book House. 1989.

three examples, out of many, to show that it is quite unscriptural to describe a deacon as an inferior office-bearer in the church," or even to apply the name only or even primarily to one who administers the funds of a church, though a deacon might be one who did so. The brother who, for instance, takes a Gospel service, gives a Bible lecture, writes a needed book, or distributes money to the poor, is a deacon in reference to his particular service. To be a *doulos* or bond-slave is a much deeper thing. Here the man is viewed more in relation to his Master, than to the service rendered. He is the personal property of his Owner. Whether his Master gives him work to do or not makes no difference. He is not his own; he must keep himself free for his Master's use. His work is never done. By night or day he is the *doulos* – the bond-slave – of his Master. The Lord Jesus was truly the *diakonos* of man. "He came not to be ministered unto, but to minister" (Matt 20. 28); but He was never man's bond-slave. He was ever in deed and in truth the bond-slave of His God – and such, too, we are called to be. Alas, how slow we are to rise to all that the name implies! Nor let us forget the Divine precept, "Ye are bought with a price," became not "bond-servants of men" (I Cor 7. 23).

(b) The second consequence of our Lord's determinate counsel was his **INCARNATION**: *"He became in the likeness of men."* These words mark the special condition in which our Divine Lord was to carry out His allotted service as the bond-servant of Jehovah. "The likeness of men"! He might conceivably have come down to the level of the archangel and have served God in the majesty of a Michael. This would have been "a self-effacement" for Him who was in the form of God; but "He took not up angels, but He took up the seed of Abraham" (Heb 2. 16), and so it behoved Him to be "made like unto His brethren," and become partaker of flesh and blood. He, the Divine Person, who had from eternity been only in the form of God, now took to Himself a perfect human nature, and became, not in appearance only, but in reality, MAN, with a real human body (Heb 10. 5), soul (John 12. 27), and spirit (Luke 23. 46). One Person, with two distinct and perfect natures, the divine and the human – never to be divided. In addition to His sovereign Divine will He had a human will, which, though perfect, was never the ultimate cause of action with Him, but was always subject to that of the Father. In the garden of Gethsemane we see the Holy and the Spotless One shrinking from contact with sin and from the consequent abandonment by a Holy God. Gethsemane was in no sense the place of sin-bearing nor of atonement, but the infinite and unutterable terrors of Golgotha no doubt pressed upon Him in the garden by vivid anticipation. It was not for Him to go forward to the Cross, like mere human heroes have met their fate, in blissful ignorance of what it would entail. Not only would He know it, as He knew all things, but that awful being who had the power of death, though not over Him, would, with all his Satanic energies, seek to bring home to that troubled soul what the cup of wrath would mean. That He was not actually drinking the cup in Gethsemane is, I believe, perfectly certain, and no less clear is it that that cup in its deepest sense was no suffering that the hand of man or the hatred of Satan could possibly inflict, but the full experience of the Divine wrath and judgment against sin which "being made sin" and "bearing our sins" on the cross would involve. The exquisite intensity of the experience of that anticipatory suffering we may gather from the words, "Being in an agony He prayed more earnestly, and His sweat was as it were great drops of blood falling down to the ground," (Luke 22. 44) along with the agonizing cry, "Father, if it be possible, let this cup pass from Me!" (Matt 26. 39). And yet never was His will more subject than at that moment, for He adds, "Nevertheless, not My will, but Thine be done." (Luke 22. 42). All this shows that though we cannot too jealously hold and assert the essential deity of our Lord Jesus Christ, we must no less forcibly hold the fundamental truth of His real and spotless humanity.

(c) The third thing involved in our Lord's determination not to insist on equality with God was His **HUMILIATION**. "Being found in fashion as a man, He humbled Himself and became obedient unto death, even the death of the cross." The word here translated "fashion" (*schema*) refers to the outward semblance of things, which may be merely transitory in character, in contrast with the word for "form" (*morphe*) which, we have seen, stands for their essential "inwardness," which cannot but be permanent. The verbs formed from these two words are an interesting study, and fully bear out the above distinction. Thus in Rom 12. 2 the Christian is exhorted not to be "conformed to this world" – that is, not to put on the outward semblance of a worldling (this is the verb compounded with *schema*), but to "be transformed [here the *morphe* verb is used] by the renewing of his mind." In 2 Cor 11. 14, where Satan is said to be "*transformed* into an angel of light," the translation is unfortunate, for it is the verb formed from the superficial word *schema* in the original, his resemblance to an angel of light being of course not inward and durable, but outward and transitory. But in 2 Cor 3. 18, where the believer is said to be "changed into the same image," it is the deep, essential *morphe* root which is used. Why then is the superficial word "*fashion* as man" (*schema*) used here? It might seem to call in question the reality of our Lord's humanity, but it does not. What it implies is that, to the world around, He seemed a simple man, and nothing more. Religious art depicts Him as a shining demigod (indeed, the conventional headcovering of even an apostle is a halo); but no ray of divine glory shone from that Face "so marred more than any man." (Isa 52. 14). To the world He was the son of Joseph and Mary, the carpetner of Nazareth, or at best the prophet of Galilee. When, in 1697, Peter the Great, in the pursuit of knowledge, worked in the garb of a simple shipwright on the quays of Amsterdam, he was still known to be the Czar, and doubtless his condescension was well appreciated at the time. It is not so difficult to take a low place, if all present know we might claim a far higher; indeed, it is possible to be proud of our humility, and

> "The pride the Devil likes the best to see
> Is the pride that apes humility."

But who could have thought that the Babe in the manger of Bethlehem was "the Child" foretold by Isaiah, whose name should be called "Wonderful, Counsellor, the Mighty God, the Everlasting Father, the Prince of Peace"? (Isa 9. 6) Yet the wise men taught of God "worshipped Him." (Matt 2.11). To the bustling crowd of temple worshippers the Infant in Simeon's arms would simply be one more "child of forty days"; to the aged saint He was "the Lord's Christ", the "Salvation that He had prepared." (Luke 2. 30, 31). So through His earthly ministry, He was weary, hungry, thirsty, and tried. He moved among men, yea, among publicans and sinners, "in fashion as a man." He neither patronised men, nor sought their suffrages. He was the meek and lowly One, who went about doing good and seeking only the glory of the Father.

All this was true of Him, but His humiliation went further. "He was obedient unto death, even the death of the cross." It has been well said, in contrast to this that "Adam was disobedient unto death." *His* death was the fruit of his disobedience, but our Lord, in obedience to the Father's commandment, "laid down His life that He might take it again." (John 10. 17). His body was a real human body, as we have seen, and capable of death, as He proved at the Cross; but a premature death during His ministry or in the garden of Gethsemane was a moral impossibility. The teaching that asserts the contrary is as derogatory to the

Person of Christ as it is contrary to the Word of God. The hand of His would-be murderers was always evaded by Divine prescience (*e.g.,* Matt 2. 13) or stayed by Divine power (*e.g.,* Luke 4. 30; John 8. 59). The fact is, death had no claim on Him. His body was not liable to dissolution in the sense of being subject to it.[3] Yet it was in order to die that He took part of flesh and blood, and though He knew full well what the cup contained. "He was obedient unto death, even the death of the cross." And so He went to Golgotha – the place of rejection, of cruel suffering, and of enduring to the utmost for righteousness' sake at the hands of man; the place of the burnt-offering where He gave Himself wholly for God, and perfectly glorified Him; the

---

[3] Questions, the idleness of which is only equalled by their irreverence, as to how different suppositious accidents would have affected our Lord's body, have been propounded by certain persons engaged, I am afraid, in heresy-hunting. To any troubled by such controversial questionings, I would venture to recommend a close adherence to the very words of Scripture; avoiding carefully all attempts at definition where Scripture is silent. Thus, for instance, Matt 2. 13 says, "Arise and take the young child ... and flee into Egypt ... For Herod will seek the young child, to destroy him." And verse 20, "Go into the land of Israel; for they are dead which sought the young child's life." And John 8. 59, "Then took they up stones to cast at Him: but Jesus hid Himself," etc. This gives us one side of the truth, and a very real side. Those who slur it over, in their eagerness to avoid error, are in more danger than they suspect of falling into the opposite heresy of Doceticism, which denies to the Lord a real body.

Now for the other side, no less important than the first. In Matt 14. 25 we see "Jesus ... walking on the sea." Again, in Mark 16. 18 we read – "They shall take up serpents; and if they drink any deadly thing, it shall not hurt them." And in Luke 10. 19 the Lord says to His disciples, "I give unto you power to tread on serpents and scorpions, and over all the power of the enemy; and nothing shall by any means hurt you," to which we may add His words in John 10. 18, "No man taketh my life from me, but I lay it down of myself."

It is difficult to see what useful purpose can be served by raising such speculative questions about the person of the Lord, even if they did not seem to raise the question as to whether God's purposes were safe in His own hands. In fact, I believe that the true answer to these speculations as to what would have ensued, had certain eventualities happened, is simply "They did not happen."

place of the sin-offering, "without the camp," (Lev 4. 12) where He had to cry, "Thou hast brought Me into the dust of death." (Psa 22. 15). It was there "He tasted death for every man" (Heb 2. 9); it was there "He became a curse" for those "who were under the law" (Gal 3. 13); it was there He "was made sin for us, that we might become the righteousness of God in Him" (2 Cor 5. 21); it was there He disanulled the power of the devil; it was there as on the scapegoat that His people's sins and transgressions were laid on Him; it was there He "by Himself purged our sins," (Heb 1. 3) and "brought in everlasting righteousness." (Dan 9. 24). In the passage before us I judge the thought is more especially the cross viewed as the place of entire submission to the will of God, the nadir of His humiliation. It was "the mind that was in Christ Jesus" which led Him to this complete submission, and in this sense we are called to be "minded as He was minded." But to the cross as the place of atonement we were never asked to go, even were we not absolutely incapable of such a thing.

It now remains to consider briefly the remaining points of this fundamental theme.

4

THE THREEFOLD REWARD – EXALTATION, DESIGNATION, AND RECOGNITION (PHIL 2. 9-11)

WE have seen that the carrying out of the Divine purpose entailed for our Lord the threefold result of renunciation, incarnation, and humiliation. We will now note the threefold reward He received from God, resulting from His humiliation.

(a) **His Exaltation:** "Wherefore God also hath highly exalted Him." Truly He is the One whom the Father delighteth to honour. He has raised Him from the dead and given Him glory, in the highest place that heaven affords, even on the Father's throne. As Son of Man He has entered into that glory He already enjoyed as Son of God, before the world began. He that "humbled Himself" has been "exalted", in contrast with that awful being "who sealed up the sum – full of wisdom and perfect in beauty," (Ezek 28. 12) and whose heart was lifted up, because of that very beauty, and whose lurid course of rebellion and of self-exaltation will only end in the lake of fire, as the most abject of God's creatures – for ever abased, as the result of his self-exaltation. But we see the self-abased Jesus, of Calvary, now "crowned with glory and honour." (Heb 2. 9).

(b) **His Designation:** "And hath given Him a Name which is above every name." "God hath made this same Jesus . . . both Lord and Christ" (Acts 2. 36). Many, if asked what this Name is that is above every name, would answer – Jesus. But surely this is not so. The name Jesus, was given by the angel before His conception, carrying with it truly in His case a special and blessed meaning, for "He shall save His people from their sins," (Matt 1. 21) though the name itself was common enough in Jewish families. The same root occurs in the names Joshua and Hosea of the Old Testament, and in Colossians 4. 11 we read of a converted Jew who bore the name of "Jesus," and was surnamed "The Just." The name "Jesus" is, indeed, as "ointment poured forth" to the affections of the redeemed, but that name was given before His incarnation, whereas the name referred to here, was granted as a special act of Divine favour after His cross and humiliation. What is the name then that is above every name, but the name of "Lord?" And this is borne out by verse 11 – "That every tongue shall confess that Jesus Christ is *Lord*." It would be well if all remembered this, and if young believers especially had it inculcated on them to speak not of "Jesus," but with the deepest reverence of "The Lord Jesus." Dead kings lose their titles. We speak of William the Conqueror, Henry 8th, but as loyal subjects of the king, it would have been normal to speak of King William or King Henry or simply "the King." Certainly no subject would dare to drop the title when in the *presence* of a living sovereign. It is to be feared that those who speak habitually of "Jesus," or "Jesus of Nazareth," and address Him, before whom "the seraphim veil their faces," as their "elder brother," have as yet a very defective view of His majesty – if, indeed, they have ever known Him as their Lord. There are a few passages in the epistles where, in order to emphasise that the One spoken of is the same who, in humble guise, walked this earth, the name Jesus appears alone – *e.g.,* Heb 2. 9, "We see Jesus," or Heb 12. 2, "Looking unto Jesus" – but in the vast majority of cases the title of "Lord" is prefixed so that the third result may follow.

(c) **His Recognition and Acclamation:** "That at the Name of Jesus every knee should bow, and every tongue confess that Jesus Christ is Lord." If in the church of Colosse one had spoken of Jesus, some might have thought the Colossian Christian of that name was referred to but all would recognise the reference at once if "The *Lord* Jesus" were mentioned. Doubtless all heaven has already acclaimed Him as Lord, and on earth all who are born of God do confess His name and recognise His rights. One day the whole universe must voluntarily or compulsorily acknowledge His claims and bow to His authority. Notice the three classes mentioned here: "Things in heaven, things in earth, and things under the earth." It has been remarked, and is of great importance if we are to avoid the deadly heresy of Universalism, that in Eph 1. 10, where it is a question of all things being "headed up in Christ," and in Col 1. 20, where it is "the reconciliation of all things to God" which is in view, the phrase "all things" is limited in two ways – first, to those who are the effective objects of the grace of God; and secondly, to things in heaven and earth. As regards the first limitation we know that there are those on earth who will, alas! never be "headed up in Christ" nor "reconciled to God." But as regards the second, we notice that here, wehre it is a question merely of submission to the Lord Jesus, "things under the earth" are included. Some have taught that what is meant by "every knee bowing in the name of Jesus" is, that all will henceforth pray and give thanks in His name; but have we any Scriptural authority for supposing that the "things in heaven" pray at all? And how is it possible in any case to conceive of the "things under the earth" (whether we take them to be, as above, "infernal beings," or with others simply "the dead") as doing so? "Offering prayer" is a thing which is only true in a very partial sense even of "things on the earth." God is represented here as conferring a special and signal honour on the Lord Jesus. I ask: Would it be adequate to interpret this as merely meaning that those in heaven, in earth, or below the earth, who pray, however few such might be, should henceforth do so in the name of Jesus? I believe the terms of the declaration are absolute, and designate not some restricted and particular class, but all in the various localities named. Besides, instead of understanding the words "in the name of Jesus" to mean "using the name of Jesus in prayer," is it not much more in consonance with the sense of the passage to understand it as meaning "in virtue of His authority"? We have frequent instances of this usage of the expression "in His name"; as, for instance, in Acts 10. 48, where Peter commands Cornelius and his friends "in the name of the Lord to be baptized". I judge then that the true sense of the passage is that, sooner or later, the entire universe will acknowledge "Jesus Christ as Lord, to the glory of God the Father." Happy those who do so now!

5

THE THREEFOLD RESPONSIBILITY ENTAILED
(PHIL 2. 12-16)

THE immediate result of all this is clearly intended to be, as stated in verse 5, "that the same mind should be in us, which was also in Christ Jesus"; but the effects of a true learning of Christ as presented to us in this remarkable passage, cannot fail to influence our Christian experience at every point.

We have seen that the carrying out of the Father's will involved on the part of Christ a threefold *renunciation,* and earned for Him a threefold *recompence*. We may say too, that what He has done entails upon us a threefold *responsibility*. Accordingly, the next paragraph begins with the deductive word "Wherefore."

First, **as to Life:** "Work out your own salvation with fear and trembling." Only ten years had elapsed since Paul was in prison at Philippi. Among those who would read these words would therefore quite possibly be the Philippian jailor of Acts 16. Well would he remember that midnight scene, and his anxious cry – when roused from the slumber of a lifetime – and the blessed answer of peace he received: "Believe on the Lord Jesus Christ, and thou shalt be saved" (v 31). Ever since that memorable night he would have known what it was to have received the salvation of his soul. Now he reads a word of different import – "Work out your own salvation." Rest not satisfied to call it your own! Make the most of it! Turn it to best account! Yield yourselves to God, "for it is He that worketh in you both to will and to do of His good pleasure" (v 13). Salvation here, as in many other passages of the New Testament, is viewed as a thing not yet complete.

Next, **as to Walk:** "Do all things without murmurings and disputings." (v 14). Murmurings and disputings are symptoms of departure from the Lord, and they occur in this moral order – first, the sin in undertone; then the sin with noise and clamour. When we read in Mark 9. 33, 34, that the Lord, in the house at Capernaum, asked, "What was it that ye disputed among yourselves by the way?" it is clear they had dropped out of line and fallen behind their Master. Had they kept rank with Him they could not, for very shame, have disputed by the way who should be the greatest. If without sufficient Scriptural reason we are falling out with our brethren by the way, is it not a sign that we too have fallen out of line with our Lord?

And lastly, **as to Testimony.** We hear much of revival in these days – and far be it from me to say it is not sadly needed. Great efforts are made in some cases to "get it up," in others to "bring it down", but without much result. May it not be that the channels are clogged by our wordliness, evil-speaking, and jealousies? O for more of the love which covers rather than comments on the failures of our brethren! And then we should be able to hold forth the Word of Life with increased power and, perhaps, with increased blessing, "in the midst of a crooked and perverse generation, among whom we shine as lights in the world." (v 15). May this be so with all the people of God while "waiting for His Son from heaven . . . who shall change the body of our humiliation that it may be fashioned like unto His glorious body according to the working whereby He is able even to subdue all things unto Himself"! (Phil 3. 21).

THE LESS INCLUDES THE GREATER

To sight, a weary Jew by Sychar's well,
And nothing more, beneath the noonday sun.
What might He have to offer, such an One?
A living draught that could all thirst dispel.
What claims assign? A prophet's power to tell
The stranger all that she had ever done,
Then stand unveiled as the anointed Son,
The Saviour God, with man content to dwell.

There is an inner and an outer guise:
The vast sea murmurs in the sea-born shell.
Not e'en a universe could quench the sighs
Of man's poor heart, their earth-bound prison cell
Infinity once shone through infant eyes,
Eternal love in Calvary's darkest spell.

WH

NOTES

NOTES

NOTES

NOTES

NOTES

NOTES

NOTES

NOTES